Developing Microcomputer Work Areas in Academic Libraries

Supplements to
Small Computers in Libraries

1. Essential Guide to dBase III+ in Libraries
   Karl Beiser
   ISBN 0-88736-064-5   1987   CIP

2. Essential Guide to Bulletin Board Systems
   Patrick R. Dewey
   ISBN 0-88736-066-1   1987   CIP

3. Microcomputers for the Online Searcher
   Ralph Alberico
   ISBN 0-88736-093-9   1987   CIP

4. Printers for Use with OCLC Workstations
   James Speed Hensinger
   ISBN 0-88736-180-3   1987   CIP

5. Developing Microcomputer Work Areas in
   Academic Libraries
   Jeannine Uppgard
   ISBN 0-88736-233-8   1988   CIP

Developing Microcomputer Work Areas in Academic Libraries

Jeannine Uppgard

Meckler

Supplement to *Small Computers in Libraries*, no. 5

Library of Congress Cataloging-in-Publication Data

Developing microcomputer work areas in academic
  libraries/edited by Jeannine Uppgard; with
  contributions by Mary Louise Brady...[et al.]
     p. cm. -- (Supplement to small computers in
  libraries; 5)
  Bibliography: p.
  Includes index.
  ISBN 0-88736-233-8 (alk. paper): $37.50
    1. Microcomputers--Library applications .
  2. Libraries, University and college--Automation.
  3. Computer-assisted instruction. 4. Educational
technology.
  I. Uppgard, Jeannine. II. Brady, Mary Louise.
  III. Series.
  Z678.93M53E78 1988   87-31232
  025.5'2777'0285--dc19   CIP

British Library Cataloguing in Publication Data

Developing microcomputer work areas in academic
  libraries
  1. Libraries, University and college--Microcomputers--
  Library applications--Great Britain
  I. Uppgard, Jeannine II. Brady, Mary Louise
  027.7'028'5   Z676.U5

  ISBN 0-88736-233-8

Meckler Corporation, 11 Ferry Lane West, Westport, CT
  06880
Meckler Ltd., Grosvenor Gardens House, Grosvenor
  Gardens, London SW1W 0BS

Printed on acid free paper
Manufactured in the United States of America

Contents

Preface

This book grew out of an interest in the topic of public access microcomputers in academic libraries based on my experience at Westfield (Massachusetts) State College. In 1983, our microcomputer lab was established to support the course, Computers in Education, and other related courses offered by the Education Department. We were also interested in developing an appropriate software collection that would complement the curriculum materials located in the Educational Resources Center.

As the facility was set up and became operational, I became interested in how other academic librarians were handling and coping with the innovations brought about by the installation of microcomputers. Some information on public access microcomputers was available at that time, but what had been published dealt almost exclusively with microcomputers in the public library.

Certainly there were other academic librarians looking for suggestions, much as I was doing. The occasion of a sabbatical leave presented itself and allowed me the opportunity to continue this inquiry in the form of a questionnaire and report, which was later published in *Small Computers in Libraries*. Several other articles and books have since been published, and the topic has been addressed at recent meetings of the American Library Association, and SCIL's Software/Computer Conference for Information Managers and Librarians.

The five cases included in this book present another opportunity for academic librarians to learn from the experiences of others. Each lab is unique, yet the cases describe situations that are frequently duplicated in one form or another in other libraries. Therefore, some general principles of operation do emerge, and the librarian/manager's point of view as presented by Peggy Seiden helps bring them together.

It has been my experience that we all benefit from sharing information with our colleagues who are struggling with the same problems in different libraries across the country. Hopefully, librarians working in the ever-changing environment of computer technology will find in this volume answers to some of their questions and suggestions for further study. I would like to thank Meckler Corporation for the opportunity to bring this information to the academic community. I am particularly grateful to the six contributors for sharing their experiences with such professionalism and expertise. It has been a pleasure working with them.

Jeannine Uppgard
September 1987

Introduction

Public access microcomputer centers in academic libraries are shaped by their host libraries and colleges and, therefore, have both similarities and differences, as do their parent institutions. The reasons for their establishment and the scope of their services give each lab unique characteristics, as can be seen in the case studies that follow. The authors have been closely involved in the establishment and the day-to-day activities of the labs and this first-hand knowledge is readily apparent in their discussions.

Why have academic libraries become a popular campus site for the location of microcomputers? Several reasons can be cited, including the library's schedule of long and regular hours, its expertise at managing special collections, and the attention it gives to security considerations. These points are recognized in the cases of the State University College at Geneseo and Raymond Walters College. Librarians are also initiating the labs in order to introduce microcomputers and software applications to students as research and learning tools. The University of Wisconsin and California Polytechnic are particularly involved with these goals, but in varying formats. Rhode Island College is especially unique because of the number of services it provides to people from outside the college community.

As plans are made and implemented for the microcomputer lab, an important concern that must be addressed is the relationship between the library and the college's computer services department. Many types of configurations are possible, ranging from total to minimal library control. A library housing a microcomputer lab, but with staff exercising little or no authority over access, services, etc., has a situation that will undoubtedly lead to many frustrating moments for librarians and students alike. However, many libraries have no staff members with sufficient technical and hardware expertise to successfully establish a lab. Some arrangement with the computer center, therefore, is a necessity especially at the outset.

Microcomputers can be wonderful, time-saving tools, but learning the subtleties of a new software package is a time-consuming and sometimes frustrating experience. Because of this, microlab patrons frequently need personal assistance. The library staff can be expected to assume additional responsibilities and more student help will need to be hired. Knowledgeable and well-trained students seem to perform the largest portion of one-to-one assistance in the labs. These can be challenging and interesting positions that students will enjoy while performing an essential service. Lab assistants will always be in demand regardless of how extensive are the workshops and training sessions conducted by faculty, computer center personnel, and/or librarians.

Among the many tasks that generally accompany the establishment of a microcomputer lab is the creation of a software collection with provisions for control and maintenance. Once again, the library staff will be asked to incorporate these additional responsibilities into existing library operations or to establish new service points to accommodate the software.

Copyright considerations will also come into play as policies are developed. Librarians are aware of the copyright laws protecting computer software and are willing to be guided by the existing laws and ethical codes when providing software programs for use in the labs. Informing lab users of their responsibilities in this area will be handled by various means, including posted signs and onscreen messages.

The microcomputer has taken its place in the academic library. Making use of this extremely versatile piece of equipment will allow for the expansion of library services to meet the ever increasing demands of a computer literate clientele. Careful planning and management will make the public access microcomputer service one that librarians can be proud of and one that students will appreciate.

Chapter One

The University of Wisconsin–Parkside

Linda Piele
Head, Public Services Division

The University of Wisconsin–Parkside, located near Lake Michigan between the cities of Kenosha and Racine, has an enrollment of 5,500 students of whom roughly one-half are part-time. Most of its students are commuters, with more than half over the age of twenty-five. Although the University offers masters degrees in business and public administration, it is primarily an undergraduate institution.

The Library/Learning Center serves as the central campus resource for both print and nonprint materials. Its three divisions (technical services, media services, and public services) are staffed by a total of nine librarians, two media professionals, and twelve paraprofessional/clerical employees. The microcomputer lab, administered by the public services division, is one level below the main, entrance level of the Library/Learning Center. This lower level also houses the library's audiovisual software collection and equipment for patron use. The lab now includes 57 microcomputers, 17 Apple IIs, 11 Apple Macintoshes, 16 IBM PCs, and 13 Zenith Z-150s.

Start-up Phase

In 1982, the university faced the need to provide its students and faculty with access to microcomputers. Requests for microcomputer labs were coming to the university administration from continuing education, the education department, and the business department. The campus computer center had shown little enthusiasm for the new technology, so the administration turned to the library.[1] The library had already agreed to house and make available to students two Apple II plus micros that a faculty member had received through a grant, so some preliminary planning was already underway. In fact, we were considering how a proposal to acquire additional microcomputers might best be made. We quickly agreed to make use of campus end-of-year funds to equip a small lab to be administered by the library.

Planning Process

The initial planning process was drastically shortened by the need to select and order equipment within two weeks—hardly ideal, but typical of life in state institutions. The chancellor designated a faculty member who had microcomputer experience to help us at this stage. After working with the library to develop tentative goals, our joint recommendation was to purchase eight Apple II plus microcomputers, one heavy-duty, dot-matrix printer, and to link all the equipment to a Corvus hard disk using the Omninet networking system. We selected the Apple II plus microcomputers because at that time they had the widest variety of software available to them and were suitable for our broad goals. The networking system would, in theory, reduce the necessity of circulating large numbers of floppy disks by making it possible to distribute much software electronically within the lab. This recommendation was accepted by the library, the university computing advisory group, and the chancellor.

Once the hardware decisions were made, we had several months to develop policies and procedures, prepare a site, train staff, etc., before the lab would open at the beginning of the fall term. An ad hoc library committee with representatives from the areas that would be most affected by this new service (acquisitions, cataloging, circulation, reference) was appointed to develop and implement plans; the faculty consultant agreed to serve on the committee as well.

Figure 1. The microcomputer lab at the University of Wisconsin–Parkside

One of our first tasks was to review and confirm our tentative goals. Those we proposed, and which the campus administration accepted, were very broad:

1. to promote campus computer literacy
2. to provide access to microcomputers and microcomputer applications for the campus community
3. to support the curriculum, except for instruction in computer programming, which would continue to use time-sharing systems.

Software Collection

We agreed that our software collection should include a variety of software types, from general applications, such as word processing, spreadsheets, and database management packages, that would support the curriculum indirectly, to instructional software that would provide more direct curriculum support. We determined that we would select only representative examples of general application packages, since we had neither unlimited funds nor the staff time necessary to support many different packages. In reviewing our collection development policy, we found that it was broadly phrased and would require no revisions.

We soon realized the full extent to which our decision to use a network to distribute software would impose special constraints. Software that is copy-protected will not work on a network, since the first step in distributing it is to copy it onto a hard disk. Although noncopy-protected software doesn't present this technical hurdle, many producers will not allow their software to be used on a network. A check of copyright law confirmed our original suspicion that we could not use the network to distribute software licensed for individual use unless we received special permission from the producer. We decided to purchase software that would work on the networking system if possible, but if a network version of a desirable package was either not available or was expensive in relation to its projected use, we would simply distribute it on floppies.

How were we going to let patrons know what software we had? Our card catalog of print and audio-visual materials was already integrated, so our inclination was to catalog and add microcomputer software to it. OCLC did not at that time have a format for microcomputer software, but we decided to go ahead and catalog our software using available AACRII guidelines and to prepare catalog cards manually. We also decided to develop a network menu that would briefly list all software by broad subject categories.[2]

We would store software and documentation behind the adjacent check-out desk and would circulate them for two hours for use only within the Library/ Learning Center. Permission would be given to faculty members to take software to classrooms for demonstrations.

Site Selection and Preparation

In selecting a site for the lab, we took into account several factors: available space, electrical power, noise, security, and proximity to an existing circulation desk and to other service points. We were fortunate in having ample space adjacent to our existing audio-visual equipment area that satisfied almost all requirements. This area was close to the check-out desk already used to circulate audio-visual software, and adding the responsibility for circulating microcomputer software would pose few problems. The microcomputers would be easily visible to staff at this desk, minimizing danger of theft and vandalism. Floor outlets with electrical power were available, as were additional floor outlets that could be used for the network wiring.

The only serious deficiency in this location was that it was not close to an existing service point that could provide help for users. The student check-out desk attendants were already busy, and their own responsibilities would not allow them to leave the desk to help users.

To prepare the site, other preparations had to be made. We decided we would adapt existing wet carrels to hold the microcomputers. Their metal legs were slightly shortened to make them 27 inches in height (one was left higher to allow for wheelchairs). We secured the equipment by installing U-bolts and using bicycle cables to lock them to the carrels. We also installed locks on the tops of the Apples to prevent users from removing cards.

Policies

Anticipating heavy demand for the microcomputers, we worried that a few users might monopolize them. To prevent this, we installed a lock that controlled the on/off switch on each microcomputer and made the keys available for two-hour check-out at the nearby check-out desk. Since a reservation system would take too much staff time, access would be on a first-come, first-served basis.

GUIDELINES FOR GROUP USE OF MICROCOMPUTERS

Microcomputers may be reserved on a first-come-first-served basis by UW-Parkside faculty/staff for use of groups in conjunction with courses and workshops sponsored by UW-P, including those sponsored by UW-Extension. Because demand for these facilities on the part of individual students, faculty, and staff is very heavy, use on a scheduled basis by groups must be somewhat restricted.

1. A maximum of 16 IBM/Zeniths, 9 Apples, or 9 Macintoshes may be reserved. Reserved sessions for the Apples and Macintoshes are limited to two hours.

2. Scheduled UW-P courses should meet regularly in their own classrooms, with group sessions on the microcomputers scheduled only as needed for hands-on instruction. It is expected that assignments will be completed by students on an individual basis at times other than those scheduled for group use.

3. Instructors are asked to minimize the length of scheduled group sessions by planning to have demonstration/lecture sessions precede or follow scheduled hands-on sessions; room D-117 may be reserved for this purpose. It is not possible, however, to reserve both Room D-117 and microcomputers for the same period.

4. There is no limit to the number of hours per day or week that may be reserved on the IBMs, but no more than 16 IBMs will be reserved for use at one time.

5. A maximum of four hours of group use (total) will be scheduled for Apple or Macintosh on any one day during fall and spring semesters. A maximum of six hours per day of group use for those areas will be scheduled during summer session and interim periods.

6. Group sessions on Apples and Macintoshes will be scheduled to allow a minimum of one hour of use by individuals between sessions.

7. Guidelines 5 and 6 do not apply when five or fewer of the microcomputers are being reserved for a group.

8. Faculty/staff member making a reservation must personally sign the log and pick up "in-use" cards at time of group use.

9. ALL RESERVATIONS NOT CLAIMED WITHIN 15 MINUTES OF THE START OF THE SCHEDULED TIME WILL BE FORFEITED UNLESS THE MICROCOMPUTER AREA STAFF IS NOTIFIED AT LEAST 2 HOURS BEFORE THE RESERVATION IS SCHEDULED TO BEGIN.

10. In some cases, a reservation request may conflict with prior reservations by individuals. The only way to be certain of avoiding such a conflict is to submit a request at least 10 days in advance.

11. All reservations are subject to approval by a Microcomputer Area Supervisor. Additionally, long-term reservations (more than two sessions) must be approved by the Director of the L/LC, and it is strongly advised that longer-term requests be placed before the beginning of the semester to help ensure that the requestor's time and equipment needs can be met.

12. Requests for use of the computers on a weekly (or more frequent) basis are subject to negotiation if a conflicting short-term request is made at a later date.

September, 1986

Figure 2. Guidelines for group use of computers

The question of whether we would allow users to play recreational games came up at this point. We decided that we would allow game playing if no one was waiting for a computer, but that anyone playing a game could be bumped by a person wanting to use the microcomputer for any purpose.

The committee knew that groups would also want to use the area for instructional sessions. We wanted to allow this type of use but did not want it to become the dominant use. Our solution was to allow groups to reserve the area, but for no more than two hours at a time; total group use would not be allowed to exceed four hours each day. See Figure 2 for the guidelines regulating the group use of the area.

Staffing and Supervision

The question of how much help users would need and how we should and could provide it was discussed at length. We had asked for and received from the university funds to hire a student assistant for twenty hours per week. He would be in the area and available to help users during most of that time, but that would leave the area unstaffed the other seventy hours a week. We felt responsible for being able to orient users to the system, show them how to insert a floppy disk, boot up, and follow menu-driven software. But we feared that users would need more help—that they might get themselves into all sorts of trouble that library staff would have neither the time nor the expertise to get them out of.

We decided that our policy would be to help users get started, but that they would have to be pretty much on their own in using application software. We prepared point-of-use instructions for such things as turning on the computer, logging onto the Omninet network, and loading a floppy disk. We also placed one Apple at the reference desk on the next floor and connected it to the network. Whenever our microcomputer assistant was not on duty, a sign in the area directed users to come to the reference desk for help.

Responsibility for supervising the area during this initial start-up phase fell to the head of the public services division. This was due in part to personal interest on her part and the fact that other staff members had hardly been exposed to microcomputers at this point. Also, since the circulation and reference units already reported to her, she was in a good position to attempt to integrate the new service into existing programs. Supervising the area would give her an opportunity to gauge the level and amount of supervision that would ultimately be desirable.

Funding

The initial funding for equipment, supplies, site preparation, twenty hours per week of student help, and the start-up software collection were provided to the library directly through the chancellor' office. Because a painful periodical-cutting exercise was still fresh in the minds of faculty members, the chancellor wanted the funding for this new service to be separate from the regular library budget. This separation would allow both the university administration and the library to reassure faculty members that funding for books and periodicals was not being diverted for this new, and to some, frivolous purpose. The chancellor assured the library that he would provide continuing funding for operating expenses on an as-needed basis.

How the Lab Grew and Changed

Each succeeding year brought new microcomputers and other equipment to the lab. In response to increasing demand by both individuals and groups, several Apple IIes and printers were added in 1983, bringing the total number to thirteen. A university-wide task force was assembled that year to address campus computing needs, among them the acute pressures on the mainframe resources administered by the computer center. Much of this pressure came from the many students taking beginning classes in BASIC programming, a requirement for business majors.

The task-force decided that it would be more appropriate to use microcomputers for this purpose and recommended that they be added to those already in the library. Although somewhat reluctant to get involved in supporting programming instruction, which had been deliberately excluded from our original goals, we agreed to do so when given assurances of additional staffing and support. Also, we suspected that the business division would soon turn to an alternative method of providing computer-literacy training for its many students, freeing these microcomputers for purposes more compatible with library goals. Thus, in January 1984, sixteen IBM PCs, each black-boxed to a printer, were added to the lab.

The task force was also concerned with how the use of microcomputers should be integrated into the curriculum. Rather than develop a special computer-literacy requirement, this group recommended that the university focus on training faculty members, who would then fit the use of microcomputers into the curriculum as appropriate. The library was called upon to help address this need as well. A special faculty/staff workroom, equipped with four Compaq microcomputers and an IBM PC/XT, was established in January of 1984, in a room adjacent to the microcomputer lab. The faculty member who had been serving as the library's consultant was given released-time to administer the workroom and to provide consulting and training for faculty and staff.

The last major expansion of the microcomputer lab came in 1985 in response to the need for better facilities for group microcomputer instruction. Although alternative campus sites were considered, the advantages of locating additional microcomputers in the library near the existing software collection and service points proved to be compelling, even for the computer center staff (who had by this time realized that they were missing the fun). Thus, thirteen Zenith Z-150s, each with its own printer, were installed. In addition, eleven Macintoshes

Figure 3. Seminar being conducted in the microcomputer lab

were added to enable students and faculty to have access to this important new microcomputer and its software. Demand for Apple IIes still continued strong, and four more were added.

As the lab expanded and as we learned more about the needs of our users, we continuously reviewed and often made changes in our original goals, policies, and staffing. Also contributing to change was the development of substantial microcomputer interest and expertise among members of the reference staff.

Change in Goals

The most important change in our goals was the addition of an instructional component. Within a few months after the lab opened in 1982, we realized that many members of the campus community—faculty, staff, and students—needed the opportunity to be introduced to the microcomputers in a group setting. To respond to this need, two librarians developed a series of two-hour, hands-on, workshops (introduction, word processing, database management, spreadsheets) that attempted to provide a very basic introduction to major applications. The following year all seven reference-instruction librarians began to participate in offering these workshops.

As librarians learned more about microcomputers, we became more aware of the potential uses of the microcomputer as an information-access tool. We reviewed the goals of our instruction program and attempted to incorporate microcomputer literacy within them. A concrete outcome was the development of a series of seminars for faculty on end-user searching, bibliography management, and note-taking.[3] A flier describing some of the seminars is reproduced in Figure 4.

Software Collection

In 1985, we evaluated the Omninet network, used to distribute software for the Apple IIs. We had encountered many practical problems in implementing and maintaining the network. The first and most critical has already been described: the lack of software designed for and/or licensed for use on the Omninet network. Another disappointment was our lack of success in using the Omninet system to share peripherals, a capability commonly offered by networks, but not easily implemented on the Omninet system. Also, although the simple software listing that we had developed and were maintaining on the network system was useful, it

THE MICRO AS A PROFESSIONAL INFORMATION TOOL:
a seminar series for faculty and staff

The Library/Learning Center will offer a series of seminars on the use of microcomputers to retrieve, organize, manipulate and present bibliographic, textual, and graphic information. The seminars will be held on Wednesdays, from 1-3 p.m., beginning March 27th. Presentations will be conceptual rather than hands-on, and some familiarity with microcomputers will be assumed of participants. (Attendance at one of the microcomputer orientation workshops previously offered by the L/LC would be sufficient preparation.) Reservations for each seminar should be made with Roberta Odegaard, x2356. If you would like to participate but cannot attend at these times, please call to indicate your interest and times you could attend; we will schedule future sessions as needed.

SEARCHING ONLINE DATABASES
Wednesday, March 27, 1-3 p.m.

Until recently, online searching of commercial databases has required knowledge of special commands and complex techniques. At UW-Parkside, this searching is currently done by librarians at the request of students, faculty, and staff, and may require one or more meetings between the searcher and requestor to achieve the best results. Participants in this seminar will be introduced to online searching, in which a microcomputer equipped with a modem is used to access remote computerized databases over telephone lines. These databases provide the researcher with quick access to large amounts of bibliographic, numeric, and textual data. The nature of such databases and the complexities involved in searching them will be described, as will the variety of search services (such as BRS Afterdark) and software packages available to help the novice access and search databases without assistance. Seminar participants will be eligible to participate in a pilot end-user searching program that the L/LC will conduct this Spring.

MANAGING BIBLIOGRAPHIES
Wednesday, April 3, 1-3 p.m.

Creating and maintaining an organized bibliography can be useful and practical. It can also be frustrating and time-consuming. Participants will be introduced to the use of specialized microcomputer software which permits the rapid and flexible storage and retrieval of items in a collected research bibliography. Examples of software usable for this purpose include both general-purpose programs such as word processors and file managers and more specialized applications such as free-form databases and specially designed bibliography managers. Particular attention will be paid to examples of the latter two software types for both Apple and IBM, and their strengths and weaknesses will be evaluated. Included in this discussion will be a program which allows the researcher to easily incorporate references from an online computerized database search into various standardized bibliographic formats (e.g., MLA, APA). A familiarity with microcomputer file management programs is not assumed, though it may be useful. Participants in the SEARCHING ONLINE DATABASES seminar will find this a natural follow-up.

ORGANIZING RESEARCH NOTES
Wednesday, April 10, 1-3 p.m.

Organizing research notes so that they can be easily retrieved for later use often takes a great deal of time and can be very cumbersome. With the aid of free-form file management and outlining programs, managing textual data stored on floppy disks can now be performed more easily. This seminar will examine the capabilities of several programs for the IBM PC and the Apple II that are suitable for managing notes, and will enable participants to decide which program is best tailored to fit their needs.

PRESENTING INFORMATION
Wednesday, April 24, 1-3 p.m.

Faculty and staff often need to present information effectively in carrying-out teaching and other responsibilities. Obtaining professional-looking products, however, has usually required careful pre-planning and lots of lead time, to say nothing of artistic skills, special materials, or expensive typesetting services. This seminar will explore the capabilities of microcomputers, printers, plotters, and software available for use in the Library/Learning Center to assist in meeting this need. Textual information in a variety of typestyles and sizes can be readily produced for many purposes, from overheads and handouts to professional-looking copy for publications. A wide variety of charts and graphs can be easily prepared, just as easily modified, and presented on papercopy or overheads.

ALL SEMINARS WILL BE HELD IN THE FACULTY/STAFF MICROCOMPUTER WORKROOM, ON THE D-1 LEVEL OF THE LIBRARY/LEARNING CENTER.

Figure 4. Promotional flier for microcomputer seminars

required a lot of staff time. Finally, after having virtually no repair problems for the first year and a half, we began to experience extended down-time. This caused real hassles, since software that was on the network was not also available in floppy format for check-out (which would have violated copyright). Thus, when the network was down, the master copy had to be retrieved and a temporary circulating copy made whenever a patron needed to use a particular piece of software. Unfortunately, our original dealer had gone out of business, and we had been left in a weak position when it came to securing technical help and repair services. Given this experience, when we added large numbers of IBM PCs in 1984, we decided not to network them. And in 1985, when the entire floor was reorganized, we decided to devote the original Apple II pluses and the network to the campus' remedial-skills program, which had been successfully using instructional courseware especially designed for the Omninet. The vendor of this software assumed responsibility for providing repair services and technical expertise.

Furniture Changes

Our original microcomputer furniture, converted wet-carrels, worked well for individual use, but were inconvenient for group use; the panels that provided privacy for individuals made it difficult for instructors to observe and communicate with groups. With the first large expansion in 1984, we were able to purchase new tables. These improved the situation, but the large, open lab still made group instruction somewhat difficult. In 1985, when additional microcomputers were purchased specifically for group instruction, we also purchased movable room dividers. By allowing us to enclose any of our microcomputer clusters, these dividers help teachers focus the attention of a group.

Policy Changes

We quickly found it necessary to re-evaluate our policy regarding game playing. When the lab opened in 1982, many students used the microcomputers for game playing, and this quickly became the dominant use of the lab. Although our policies stated that game players could be bumped, we found that few patrons were aggressive in asserting their rights. And the noisy atmosphere created by the players seemed to discourage serious would-be users, especially anxious novices. As a result, we banned all recreational games after the first few months. With the present heavy demand on lab resources, game playing simply no longer seems to be an issue.

At the time of the 1984 expansion, we re-evaluated our microcomputer access policies. The key system had worked well in many respects, but as we added more microcomputers, we found that desk attendants were spending an inordinate amount of time simply checking microcomputer keys in and out. Furthermore, the system created something of a bottle-neck for users, who had to wait in line during busy periods. Although we were going to be able to hire many more student employees to staff the area, we wanted them to spend most of their time helping users rather than doing clerical chores.

We decided to try to design a new system that would provide some measure of control, especially during busy periods, but that would be largely self-service. Our solution was a self-service log, on which users sign themselves up for a particular machine. Up to one-third of the machines may be reserved in advance, but these reservations must be made in person and through the microcomputer assistant on duty. Microcomputer assistants also maintain a waiting list during busy periods. This system satisfies our primary goal, which is to provide some measure of control using a minimum of staff time. Its major deficiency is that not all users bother to sign in, especially during relatively low-use periods, rendering our use statistics incomplete.

Whether to keep our printers supplied with paper became an issue in 1985. We had been providing paper up until that time but had become increasingly appalled at the cost and the amount of wastage. With some misgivings, we declared an end to free paper and have been pleased with the results. After a bit of grousing, users became accustomed to purchasing paper at the book store and loading it themselves. To our surprise, printers have not been damaged more frequently by users ineptly loading paper than they were previously. We do make a box of scrap paper available.

Staffing and Supervision Changes

Our initial concern that users would need more help than we could provide proved to be well-founded, but the problem was less serious than we had feared. In the first place, those with problems learned to come during the twenty hours per week our assistant was on duty. Second, our users helped each other. Those having difficulty printing, for example, were likely to find a more experienced user willing to help them out.

However, as the lab grew in size and use, it became clear that we needed more staff. Not only did our users need more help, but the network had to be maintained, and all new software had to be checked, configured, and backed-up. These procedures turned out to be quite time-consuming, and in 1983, the chancellor agreed to increase our student help allowance to forty hours per week.

With the 1984 expansion, we obtained funding for 100 hours per week of student help and were given temporary funding for a half-time paraprofessional. (This position later became permanent, but only through a re-allocation of library staff.) By this time, it had become clear that supervising the daily operations of the lab was occupying too much of the time of the head of the public services division and that it was time to delegate these responsibilities. For six months, we experimented with having the microcomputer assistants report directly to the head of the circulation department, who had acquired much interest and expertise in using microcomputers. The half-time paraprofessional became her assistant. Unfortunately, this arrangement put too much stress on the circulation department, which already had a full quota of responsibilities.

Our ultimate solution to the supervision problem was to designate one of the reference-instruction librarian positions as microcomputer services coordinator. This position provides general coordination, while the half-time paraprofessional provides day-to-day supervision. This solution is consistent with the organization of the public services division, in which individual reference-instruction librarians coordinate one or more services (for example, reference, instruction, online searching). The microcomputer coordination responsibilities require about 35 percent of the coordinator's time.

The faculty/staff workroom evolved in terms both of staffing and purpose. With this area helping faculty and staff with microcomputers and the computer center responsible for helping them with questions related to large computers, users sometimes weren't sure when to go where. Projects that might best be done on a large computer were being done on a micro and vice-versa. In 1985, the computer center took the initiative in developing a proposal for a computing support center that would include terminals to campus mainframe systems as well as the microcomputer resources already available to faculty/staff in the workroom. One help desk would handle questions for both types of systems, and the center's staff would include both the faculty microcomputer consultant who had been working with the library and the academic computing consultant from the computer center. This proposal was accepted by all parties, terminals were added to the workroom, and its name was changed to the computing support center. Although the staffing of the center has since changed, the concept remains the same and has worked well.

Another staffing change was the assignment of responsibility for repair of microcomputer equipment to the library's audio-visual technician in the media services division. Previously, one of our student microcomputer assistants had been responsible for diagnosing repair problems and arranging for them to be sent off campus, if necessary. This had worked reasonably well, but a permanent staff member with general technical expertise was needed to oversee the process. The technician was sent for several days of training in microcomputer maintenance in 1986 before taking on this new responsibility.

Funding

The chancellor funded the microcomputer lab directly from his office on an as-needed basis until his resignation and departure from the university in 1985. Before he left, he attempted to ensure continued funding for the program by making it a separate item in the university budget. The library/learning center now receives the following annual funding for the program:

- $13,000 for supplies and expenses
- $8,500 for software
- $15,000 for student help

Although this funding covered virtually all expenses for materials and student help, the library contributes much additional staff time.

Summary

Developing the microcomputer lab and its services challenged and excited the staff and brought them opportunities for professional growth. The enthusiasm of our users was infectious, and their appreciation gratifying. Further, the library's leadership in developing these new services and integrating them into the library brought new respect from university administrators.

At the same time, it has been a lot of work, and library staff have sometimes found their enthusiasm waning, even turning to burn-out. Our users' needs have sometimes seemed overwhelming; they were not always appreciative, and we were on occasion frustrated.

Recent budget and staff cuts are forcing us to re-evaluate all library activities and take a fresh look at our long-term goals. Such evaluation may well be increasingly necessary in the future, as our desire to explore and exploit new information technologies runs up against the realities of limited staff time. In one sense, perhaps our experience in developing our microcomputer lab and its services can best be seen as good practice for such a future.

Notes

1. For background on this decision, see Allan E. Guskin, Carla J. Stoffle, and Barbara E. Baruth, "Library Future Shock: The Microcomputer Revolution and the New Role of the Library," *College and Research Libraries* 45 (May 1984): 177–87.

2. This menu is described in more detail in Linda J. Piele, "Circulating Microcomputer Software," *Access: Microcomputers in Libraries* 2 (October 1982): 7–8, 20–23.

3. This instructional program is described in Linda J. Piele, Judith Pryor, and Harold W. Tuckett, "Teaching Microcomputer Literacy: New Roles for Academic Librarians," *College and Research Libraries* 47 (July 1986): 374–78.

Chapter Two

State University of New York at Geneseo

Paul MacLean, Managing Librarian

The microcomputer lab in Fraser Library, SUNY College at Geneseo, was installed during the summer of 1983 and housed twenty-two Apple IIe and two IBM PC computers. The facility has grown to be three rooms with twenty-four IBM PCs, forty-two Apple IIes, one Apple IIgs, and ten Macintosh computers, as well as thirty-six printers. It is the college's central and largest collection of microcomputers.

The College

SUNY Geneseo is a liberal arts college, one of twelve in the State University of New York system. The college overlooks the Genesee River Valley 30 miles south of Rochester. About 4,900 full-time students are enrolled, one quarter of whom are in the business school's degree programs in accounting, management science, and economics. A program leading to the B.A. degree in computer science was established in 1984, and it was partly to support this that the College installed its first microcomputer lab in Fraser Library.

Another stimulus to creating the microcomputer lab was the State University of New York's "Appropriation for the Improvement of Student Access to Computer Instruction," first made in 1983, and based on a $25 per student fee in a $300 tuition increase made that year. Geneseo received $116,342 from SUNY's overall $3.9 million appropriation. These annual appropriations for what is now called the "Student Computing Access Program" (SCAP) have continued to provide for the maintenance and expansion of academic computing facilities at Geneseo. These include a Burroughs A-10D mainframe computer, a Digital VAX 8530, a Digital MicroVAX II, and about four hundred microcomputers, in addition to those in Fraser Library, located in mini-microlabs and offices throughout the campus. The SCAP money has been augmented by academic equipment replacement funds from the Office of Academic Affairs.

Until 1983, Geneseo maintained a school of library and information science, and it was the library school that in early 1982 purchased the first microcomputer for student instruction. This was an Apple II Plus (48K) and the only software was DOS 3.3, BASIC, and Visicalc. Before this, the college relied mostly on a Burroughs mainframe computer, with terminals located around campus, for both administrative and academic computing.

Planning, Site Preparation, and Hardware

The decision to purchase microcomputers was made in the office of academic affairs, which oversees the management of resources for academic computing. An assistant vice-president for academic affairs (AVPAA) planned and coordinated the establishment of the facility. He appointed a microcomputing committee of faculty from various academic areas to assist him. To the AVPAA, the library seemed like an ideal location for the lab. It could offer security, service, and many available hours. As well as providing space for the machines, it was envisioned that the library could circulate software and documentation as part of normal operations at the reserve desk.

Fraser Library, the college's main library from 1956 until 1966, and now a branch serving the disciplines of business, computer science, and mathematics, offered the additional advantages of being somewhat underutilized, having an available classroom, and being located in the same building as the computer science department. Fraser Library served the library school from 1967, when the college's new main library opened, until it was eliminated in 1983. Classroom and office space once used by the library school now serves the expanding computer science department. Fraser Library occupies about 13,500 square feet on the second floor of the Fraser Building, and houses about 40,000 book and periodical volumes. It is staffed by a managing/reference librarian, an afternoon/evening reference librarian, a library clerk, and fifteen student assistants. Most of the library's technical support is provided by the main library, which employs thirteen librarians, fifteen support staff, and about forty student assistants.

It was the AVPAA's desire to spend money on machines and not on furniture, so he rounded up ten identical 3x5-foot wooden tables and associated chairs dating from the 1950s. In the 800-square–foot classroom, the tables were fastened together in groups of five to form two 5x15-foot peninsulas, each capable of holding ten computers and peripherals. Two 3x8-foot tables of the same style were placed along one wall to hold two computers and a printer each. College electricians provided additional power and electrical lines into the room, and installed strips of "plugmold" along the center of each group of tables and along the wall edge of the larger tables. Because it was believed the temperature needed to be controlled, carpenters rebuilt three windows to make them suitable for air conditioners transferred from other locations. Several sections of wall shelving were moved to other areas of the building. When the computers arrived they were unpacked and set up one summer morning by the AVPAA, a few faculty with Apple experience, and the manager of academic computing.

Use of the new microcomputers was light at first, but at the end of the first year people were writing their names on the blackboard to create an informal waiting list. To continue a planned phasing in of additional computers, the following summer (1984) a 1,850-square–foot room housing the library's children's and young adult collection, which had remained in Fraser Library for use by students in the Library School, was divided into two smaller rooms. A soundproof wall with a door was constructed to separate them. The 16,000-volume collection was reduced to 10,000 by weeding and temporarily compressed into one room. The other was used for an additional twenty-four Apple IIe computers. Again, 1950s vintage wooden tables were combined in various ways to support computers, printers, and disk drives. Electricians installed a new breaker box to bring in addi-

Figure 5. The Apple IIe and Macintosh lab at Fraser Library

tional power and twelve new circuits. Air conditioning was no longer considered essential and was not provided.

The next summer (1985) the children's collection was moved to the main library. The door connecting the vacated room with the main reading room, a quiet study area, was replaced with a soundproof, emergency-exit only door. In the transformation of these rooms a number of built-in stacks and freestanding shelves were relocated to other areas in the library or college.

To provide for a separate IBM lab, during the 1986 winter intersession, the twenty-two original Apple IIes were moved into the empty room next to the other Apple computers. To make all these machines equivalent, the 6502 microprocessors in the original Apple IIe computers were replaced with 65C02 chips which came in the newer, enhanced Apple IIes. All of the Apple IIes have 128K of RAM memory, with the additional 64K provided either by an extended 80-column text card or an extended 80-column text/AppleColor adaptor card. Each computer has two Apple Disk II drives, and there is an even distribution of color and monochrome monitors. The Apple IIes are served by nineteen Okidata Microline 92 printers connected through Okidata Apple Plug 'N Play Kits, dual mode parallel interface cards, which are left switched to intelligent mode. Most printers serve two computers through a Mikon Technologies Data Switch. All of these printers are on stands which permit feeding paper from underneath.

After the Apple IIes were moved, twenty-two IBM XTs were added to the two IBM PCs in the original lab. These are all 256K machines, except for four which have been expanded to 640K and equipped with a Microsoft mouse. Each of the IBM machines has two floppy disk drives and most have color monitors. Nine are connected to printers: four Okidata Microline 92, four Okidata Microline 192 and, one IBM Graphics printer. The Okidatas emulate an IBM Graphics printer.

Ten Macintosh computers, mostly 512K enhanced models with external drives, were added a few at a time to the Apple area. These, and the recently acquired Apple IIgs, are served by Apple ImageWriter printers.

All of the computers, printers, and monitors have short, steel cables attached by college staff. These cables terminate in a small loop through which a longer cable is passed and then locked to the tables. No equipment has been stolen from any of the rooms in Fraser Library.

Staffing and Policies

Responsibility for the operation of the microlab was initially given to the department of computer science, but after six months was transferred to the computer center, and more specifically to the manager of academic computing. A programmer-analyst position was added, making an academic computing staff of two within the overall computer center professional staff of seven. The academic computing staff is strengthened by a group of twenty student consultants.

The relationship between the library staff and the academic computing staff has been a friendly, informal, and cooperative effort to support the new service, but there has been confusion about librarians' roles in assisting microcomputer users. This was somewhat clarified in 1984, when the director of college libraries asked Fraser Library's managing librarian to make a written determination of the relationship between library staff and computer facilities and users in Fraser Library. This policy is as follows:

> The computing facilities in Fraser Library are the responsibility of Computer Center staff, but the nature and location of the computers necessarily involve Library staff in a combined effort to provide user assistance and support.
> Computer Center staff have primary responsibility for user assistance. Computer Center staff are responsible for scheduling consul-

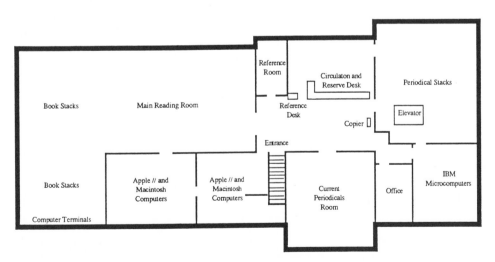

Figure 6. Floor plan of Fraser Library, SUNY–Geneseo

tants, maintaining computers and their peripherals, and for overall technical support.

Library staff are responsible for the organization and circulation of microcomputer software selected and provided by various College offices and departments. It is expected that librarians will have some knowledge of the intellectual content of these materials and be familiar with the various means of making this information available to users. Librarians will provide help, when it is sought, in a manner analogous to the way help is given to users of other library facilities and resources.

This policy was kept intentionally general in order to preserve maximum opportunities for library staff to participate in helping computer users, and perhaps that is why it has not resolved all the issues raised by the the presence of public access microcomputers in the library.

A fundamental question remains: should reference librarians in a library with public microcomputers be expected to help microcomputer users with their everyday queries, or should they stick to working with library users whose needs relate to traditional library materials—reference books, card catalogs, periodical indexes, and so on? Or, looked at another way, can reference librarians be expected not to help library users who ask questions related to their use of microcomputers?

Students come to the reference desk, where it is hoped they will encounter someone with a keen desire and sufficient knowledge to help. What difference does it make whether they come from the periodicals room or the microcomputer room? In fact, students using microcomputers may concurrently be using other library resources. Each positive interaction at the reference desk benefits those involved and confirms that it is a good place to seek assistance. Reference librarians will each bring their own attitudes, inclinations, knowledge, and abilities to assisting users of microcomputers.

Librarians at Fraser Library have acquired their knowledge in various ways. Most important has been actually using the different microcomputers and software to accomplish a large number of library-related tasks. Learning to do this requires the motivation to study manuals, read the relevant periodicals, take courses, attend training sessions, and seek help from other people at the college.

During the past year, librarians recorded giving help with 531 questions involving the use of computers, and there were at least as many unrecorded assists. Some questions are basic and routine, such as how to load paper in the printers, while others are difficult and might require some research to answer. Often, students could be referred to an appropriate manual, but usually they only need and want direct help in overcoming the immediate problem. Usually, suggestions to solve the various problems can be based on experience accumulated in similar situations.

Librarians at Geneseo do not have a formal instructional role in relation to microcomputers or software. This teaching is done by faculty in regular college classes and by computer center staff who offer a variety of short courses and special classes. Librarians have helped maintain the two locked display cases installed in each lab to serve as bulletin boards and locations for instructional displays.

During one semester, academic computing tried scheduling student consultants to be in the microcomputer labs at various times. This was unsuccessful because the consultants were not easily visible to users, were difficult to supervise by academic computing, which is located in another building, and were not consistently able to help. Student consultants are presently available in the computer center, which is a two-minute walk from the library.

Figure 7. Circulation desk showing software library cases

Access to the microcomputers is on the same basis as the rest of the library, which is open to the public eighty-seven hours a week during the academic year. Except for the last few weeks of each semester, machines are usually available without waiting.

In 1986, academic computing issued a revised policy on reservation of the microcomputers by instructors. This was partly in response to the practice of some faculty to reserve one of the labs for classes on a weekly basis. The present policy is that:

> The microcomputers in Fraser Library may be reserved by instructors for the purpose of introducing students to new course material using microcomputers. Instructors should try to develop lab presentations that do not require more than one class period to complete. The monthly reservation schedules are posted outside the labs so that students can plan their work around the closed reserved sessions. In order to provide ample notification to the many students dependent upon the equipment, reservation should be made at least one week before the room is needed.
>
> Microcomputer labs will not be available as the site for regularly scheduled semester classes. An instructor may use each lab no more than four times per course.
>
> The microlabs may be available for special courses or seminars during intersession periods and summer. Proposals for any extended scheduling should be discussed well in advance with the Computer Center staff.
>
> Multiple copies of some software are available at the circulation desk at Fraser Library. Instructors are responsible for legally providing software for their lab presentations.
>
> Reservations should be made and questions directed to Academic Computing.

There is no question that people may be inconvenienced when a lab is reserved. The divided Apple lab helps prevent this, because some of these machines are always available.

Users of printers must provide and load their own paper. Keeping the printers loaded with paper, not in a locked source, was tried, but discontinued when the supply was exhausted much more quickly than expected.

Software

Fraser Library has at the reserve desk about 165 software titles: 116 for the Apple IIe, 20 for the Macintosh, and 29 for the IBM PC. Multiple copies of some programs bring the number of circulating units to three hundred. For example, there are 28 copies of Appleworks, 14 of Lotus 1-2-3, and 11 of Macwrite; but only one copy of dBase III Plus, Microsoft Word, and Stickybear ABC.

During the past year, there were about 35,000 loans of software and manuals—mostly software. This compares with regular course reserve circulation of 9,600 items at Fraser Library and 34,000 at the main library. Regular four-week circulation at Fraser Library was 6,500 books, and 85,000 at the main library. Software is lent for two-hour periods and may be taken outside the library to any of the other microcomputer locations. To provide for protection of the disks from snowbanks, mud puddles, and other hazards, they are packaged in beige Minikasette/10 Library Cases designed to hold up to ten disks. These cases also work adequately for 3.5-inch disks. Labels, which for some of the multiple copies are color coded, are put on the "spines" of the cases.

The software collection has grown to occupy about 50 feet of shelving beneath the reserve circulation counter. These deep shelves were modified by attaching backboards at the appropriate depth to help keep the cases arranged neatly. Computer and software manuals occupy twelve shelves adjacent to twelve shelves of other books in the course reserve collection.

The same card and pocket system used to control the circulation of other library materials is used for software. A pocket is glued to the envelope of one disk in each package. For 3.5-inch disks no pocket is used and the card is just put in the case with the disks, which seems to work more easily in any case. Gluing the pocket onto disk jackets derived from the analogy with books, and from the initial method used to house and circulate software when disks were kept in hanging folders in the vertical file also used for course reserve readings.

Borrowers are required to leave an ID, which is clipped to the card identifying the item borrowed, and on which they have written their name and ID number. This is the same procedure used for all reserve circulations, except that on each card used for charging software is stamped the warning that:

The Copyright Law of the United States governs copying of copyrighted material, including software, with automated systems. Persons using the equipment are liable for infringements.

Because it is somewhat cumbersome to open and close the library cases each time software is borrowed or returned, a trial was made for some of the most frequently used items of affixing the pocket to the outside of the cases. This made circulation at the desk more efficient, but also resulted in library staff not being aware when cases were returned with disks missing. This sometimes happens even when the case is opened, especially if the package includes more than one disk. It also may not be noticed when borrowers inadvertently return their own disks in place of a library disk.

Software on reserve for use in the microcomputer labs has been selected and acquired mainly through three channels: the office of academic affairs in consultation with academic computing, various academic departments, and the libraries. (Some software comes with purchased hardware and some has been developed by faculty and staff of the college.) As examples, the office of academic affairs, hoping to standardize Appleworks as the word-processing program used by students, purchased several "ten-packs" of this program. The education department purchased a dozen or so programs for its students to use in assessing how computers and software might be used in schools. The libraries have acquired software selected by some academic departments that is purchased with money otherwise budgeted for their books. Whenever possible, archival back-up copies of software are made and stored. Usually this is done by the purchaser, although the academic computing department often does this for academic departments. Damaged software is returned to the appropriate location for repair.

The academic computing department attempts to maintain a database of all microcomputer software at the college. Accessible as a public "help" file on the mainframe computer, this database presently lists some 300 items, and gives the location and developer for each.

Fraser Library uses a database program to maintain printed lists of what software and documentation is available at the reserve desk. Separate lists for each type of computer are kept at the reserve desk and in the microcomputer labs. Any software actually acquired by the libraries is cataloged using the MARC format on OCLC. Classification numbers beginning with the code "software" are assigned, and a special subject heading, "Computer Software Collection," is added. This provides a way to see the library's collection, now about sixty titles, when consulting the card catalog.

Pros and Cons of a Public Access Microcomputer Lab

The computers in Fraser Library are used predominantly for word processing. From the student's point of view, the major benefit of using these computers may only be enjoying the significant advantages, competitive and otherwise, in creating written products. This leads some to wonder if microcomputer labs are not glorified typing rooms, portending a time when most students will have their own computer, software, and printer. Today's labs may be looked back on primarily as bridges to such a computer-rich future.

The paperless society is often heralded, but now the primary product of the computers in Fraser Library is a printed document, and printers are the chief source of complaints from users. They are also a source of bothersome noise. Most complaints result from ribbons that no longer produce dark copy, and although student consultants from academic computing put in new ribbons every two or three weeks, at a cost of about $10 a month per printer, it is still often difficult to find one that will produce the quality desired.

In the past year, an Apple LaserWriter printer was installed in the computer center, and the near typeset printing provided by this machine has greatly increased some users' expectations. This LaserWriter has been especially sought out for printing resumes and job-application cover letters. Plans have been made to install at least one more LaserWriter in the computer center, and to institute a per page charge for using it. This printer will be networked with various computers, and will have a controller attached to accept magnetically encoded vending cards. A printing room in the computer center will include a variety of other printers for producing high-quality copy.

Fraser Library's microcomputers also receive significant use for specific course assignments, or computer-assisted instruction, in subjects such as geography, chemistry, physics, biology, mathematics, accounting, management science, computer science, special and elementary education, sociology, psychology, and art. Each semester students and others sit down at a computer for the first time, often alone, and with little, if any, previous guidance. Self-teaching and peer teaching are probably the predominant and best ways of beginning to learn. But at various points in their progress a significant number of these users will seek and receive help from library staff. Giving this assistance often requires working in no-man's land, outside the defined discipline of librarianship.

Four years is a long time in the microcomputer industry, but quite brief in the life of an institution. SUNY Geneseo has made a significant commitment to providing microcomputer facilities. The machines in Fraser Library have contributed to making it a more active and interesting place, both for staff and users. They are in part the cause of a doubling in four years of the number of people entering the library. They have undoubtedly helped the college attract excellent students.

From a librarian's point of view, it will not be long before microcomputers are a major intermediary for information seeking in libraries. If today's machines or their descendants do not become networked to information sources, they may be needed as "information readers." For example, libraries now installing CD-ROM information sources consider it necessary to attach printers to these workstations. But perhaps such key access stations will be in too much demand to afford anything but the rapid capture of information, which could then be studied at another computer. Magnetic recording offers the additional advantage that data can be easily available for use in word processing and other programs. The time may be coming when more and more students will no longer have "papers" to "hand in," but will be doing the equivalent electronically.

Chapter Three

Raymond Walters College at the University of Cincinnati

Lisa Camardo, Coordinator of Computer Support Services

Raymond Walters College is one of the eighteen colleges and divisions that make up the University of Cincinnati. Located in a suburban setting, Raymond Walters was the first two-year general and technical college in the state of Ohio. Currently, there are over 3,500 commuting students attending classes in a variety of curriculum areas, including dental hygiene, nursing, business, and library/instructional media technology. A number of special laboratories exist throughout the college to provide hands-on experience in physics experiments, microbiology, computer science, and instructional television. The college offers thirty-six associate degree programs, such as: commercial art, nuclear medicine technology, accounting, office administration, and word processing.

In 1985, the college received capital funding from the State of Ohio, which was used as the initial start-up cost for purchasing computer hardware. A committee made up of college administrators and academic department heads was formed to make decisions about the allocation of these funds. The committee had three major initial concerns to contend with: spatial planning, staffing, and use and development. From the committee, subcommittees were formed to deal with specific concerns, such as the hardware configuration, student needs, and faculty needs. One decision, however, had to be made by the nucleus of this committee: Who would be responsible for this facility?

After careful consideration of the overall needs of the college, the decision was made to put this new facility in the hands of the library staff. Since the library is considered the "information center" of the college, the new computers would become part of the library's services. And so the scenario begins, and a computer laboratory is born!

Microcomputer Lab

The IBM Microcomputer Lab was established at Raymond Walters College in 1985 to provide access to computers and software programs for all members of the college community. The Lab, consisting of thirty IBM PCs, is administered through the library's media services department so that it remains accessible to the entire college community on an equal basis. The initial concept for planning and operating such a facility mirrored the paradigm of a traditional library reserve room where materials and the necessary retrieval equipment would be housed under the supervision of staff and open for patron use on a noncirculating basis.

Thrusting a room full of microcomputers into the library created as many problems for the library staff as the facility was intended to rectify for students and faculty. The first signs of inexperience surfaced when a semitrailer pulled up, laden with the individually packaged IBM CPUs, monitors, keyboards, printers, and other peripherals. The closet set aside for temporary storage of the equipment just would not do.

This experience led to quick consideration of a number of other factors affecting the design and installation of the lab equipment and formulation of procedures and policies. Since the facility could not be physically housed in the library proper, a large, double-classroom space was appropriated for use as the microcomputer lab.

Figure 8. The IBM Microcomputer Lab at Raymond Walters College

At this point, the spatial planning and immediate concerns included such items as:

- adequate electricity and grounding
- appropriate placement of outlets
- containment for electrical wires and cables
- sufficient support for hardware with adequate work space
- placement and arrangement of hardware within the facility
- storage of software and related materials
- security
- aquisition of office equipment and furniture
- installation of telephone lines

Most of these problems were resolved by the maintenance staff in the college and some outside professionals who installed phone lines and supplied tables, chairs, cabinets, and other office items. The result was a thirty-unit microcomputer lab. Each computer had expanded memory up to 512K, two floppy disk drives, and a monochrome monitor able to display high-resolution graphics. Every four units shared a graphics printer, which could be activated through a central switch box. It was quite an impressive arrangement for a small college library. (See Figure 9 for the diagram of the microcomputer lab.)

With the hardware in place, a full-time staff member was needed to get the facility operational and somehow encourage its use. So the college hired me as the microcomputer lab manager. (Note: The lab manager should have been hired long before this point. Many future problems could have been avoided had a computer expert been on the initial planning committee for such a facility.)

Planning for Service

The first order of business I needed to attend to was the assessment of college needs. Since most of the faculty had never used computers to supplement their classroom instruction, I developed a questionnaire to determine what software would best fit their teaching. Actually, the responses reflected their grave inexperience and lack of knowledge of the potential resources available to them. One faculty member who had a good amount of experience with microcomputers donated to the library ten copies of a commercial spreadsheet and some training materials which he had received from a grant. Other than these few items, the facility was not equipped with any software. So I took it upon myself to purchase some very simple software applications including word processing and a variety of public domain utilities, data bases, and games. With that, the facility opened.

On paper, the initial concept for the lab as a library reserve facility appeared sound. However, in practice, it became evident that this paradigm was not adequate. An extremely high number of patrons with various programming needs and software applications proved to require extensive, individualized assistance from the staff. This led to a revision of how the lab operation was viewed. Rather than perceiving it as a reserve facility, it evolved into an instructional facility focusing on microcomputer software applications in a variety of curriculum areas.

IBM Microcomputer Laboratory
Raymond Walters College

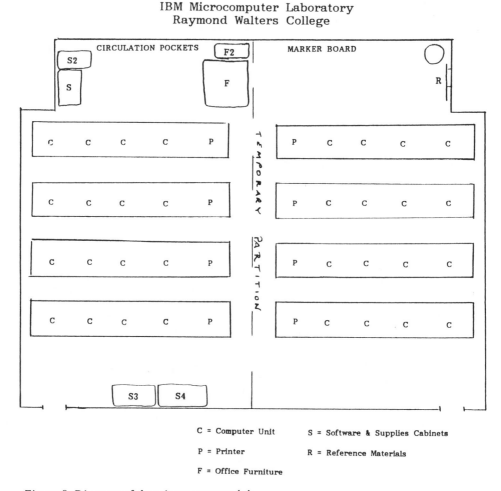

C = Computer Unit   S = Software & Supplies Cabinets

P = Printer   R = Reference Materials

F = Office Furniture

Figure 9. Diagram of the microcomputer lab

Realization of this need for individualized instruction for patrons impacted upon the daily functioning of the lab in a number of important ways:

    1. Increasing amounts of staff time were devoted to direct instruction.

    2. A need for trained staff assistants developed.

    3. The facility was being used part-time as a classroom-style learning environment, which was completely unacceptable, based on the initial concept.

In order to minimize the latter problem, a portable, monochrome computer projector was purchased to allow one computer, placed on a rolling cart, to serve as a primary instructional tool in a regular classroom, thus keeping the lab facility available for normal patron use as originally intended. However, as the number of classes integrating computer-assisted instruction into their curriculum increased, so did the instructors' desire to conduct class meetings in the facility on a regular basis.

At first, this was very simple to accommodate. Since the room was a double classroom, there was a temporary partition that formed a wall splitting the facility into two halves. Now a formal class could meet on one side of the lab and the other side would remain available for individual patron use.

Funding

As the faculty's needs changed, more software was evaluated and eventually purchased by the library for the facility. Funding for additional software was provided by the already existing library materials budget. During the first full fiscal year that the lab was open, over $10,000 was spent on software alone. The strain on the library materials budget was great. Subsequently, special funds and left-over money from other college budgets were used to purchase the new and more expensive software materials. To cover the ongoing cost of supplies needed for the printers and some preventative maintenance, another fund was set up containing only $2,000 for each year. With this restraint, I was required to spend many hours researching vendor prices and negotiating costs over the telephone. I was under great pressure to purchase only those items that were cost effective but still good in quality.

When purchasing new software, there are a number of steps which, when followed, can and will help any facility to get the most out of the software purchased. To begin, survey the faculty, or at least make them aware of the purchase. Many times, two different manufacturers will offer similar products (e.g., word processing), and a consensus of faculty opinions will minimize the purchasing of equivalent software. I have found that, if asked to suggest a particular software title, faculty will request an application with which they are already familiar, or one which a friend has recommended. With the number of titles available, this could get very expensive. Therefore, when a request for a new package is brought to my attention, I let the other faculty members who might be interested in using such an application know that one is being considered for purchase. If possible, the lab manager should make arrangements with the vendor or publisher to preview the programs and accompanying materials before confirming their purchase. One problem with this practice is that not all faculty members will be able to spend time looking at the package during the preview period, and ultimately the evaluation process is all for naught.

After a time, our library had acquired a sizable software collection of approximately seventy titles (mainly because I didn't follow my own advice about surveying the faculty in advance). Then came the need to teach the interested parties how to use the packages they had requested. I began holding in-service workshops in the lab for faculty members either considering the use of a program in their class or having a general interest. Here, too, it isn't as easy as it sounds to get even ten people to agree on one time for the workshop. Eventually, I gave up and tried another tactic, which I use to this day. When a new software package arrives, I simplify the "Getting Started" instructions and reference cards to a one-page hand-out that can suffice for the students to get started working with it. This at least assures me that everyone has the same starting point and, if individual instructors differ in the information they deem important for their students, complete reference manuals are available as well as personal assistance from the staff.

Scheduling the Lab for a Class

As the lab began to grow, so did the conflicting needs of the various departmental uses of the facility. Instructors found that they couldn't just bring a class to the lab and be guaranteed access to enough computers to accommodate their students. Therefore, a scheduling system was set up and mailed to each faculty member. Using a weekly grid, instructors could simply fill in their names at the time slot they wanted to reserve. When the grids were returned, it was very easy to spot the conflicts and work them out before the academic quarter began.

This scheduling process ironed out the problem of holding classes at the lab. It also eliminated the fear that patrons had about not being able to complete homework assignments because a class was using all the lab computers. The master schedule was posted just outside the lab doors and students as well as other instructors could refer to it without disrupting the daily operation of the lab.

Soon we found that it would be best to remove a couple of units and set up a computer workstation in the library proper. This way, if the lab was full, students could still have access to an IBM PC and a graphics printer. Later, these computers would serve as the public access computers for the college. Anyone in the community can use the library computers; however, access to software and support is limited to registered students only.

Policies and Lab Cards

My experience has always been that all new computer users, no matter what their age might be, are like children learning something new for the first time. Their inhibitions and frustrations are great in the beginning. Therefore, the policies that they are expected to follow should be small in number and enforced upon all patrons equally. Also, everyone needs to have been told exactly what those policies are. At Raymond Walters, the lab policies are presented in three ways:

1. through the use of large posters hung around the lab
2. on a printed Information Card, which briefly covers policies, support provided, student access to the lab, and simplified operating instructions for the printers and disk drives
3. through an instructional videotape, produced by the director of media services and myself, explaining the rules, software circulation procedures, and basic machine operation of the IBM PCs and peripherals.

All registered students who are planning to use the IBM microcomputer lab for classwork or personal use must view the forty-minute minute videotape and be issued a blue Lab Card and an Information Card. These two sources provide every lab patron with the ground-level information needed to begin working on the computers. It has also alleviated the constant repetition of explaining basic instructions to each new user in the lab.

The policies of the lab are simple:

1. Copying software is prohibited.
2. No eating, drinking, or smoking is allowed in the facility.
3. Don't leave printers unattended while in operation.

4. No software can be taken from the lab.
5. Patrons must present their Lab Card each time they use the lab.

Software Circulation

All commercial software is available for use by patrons in the lab only. Students may obtain software by presenting their Lab Card to the lab attendant and signing the circulation card attached to the desired package. The Lab Card is held by the attendant until all materials on loan have been returned. Simplified instructions of the start-up procedures for each package are available for patrons in the lab.

Faculty and staff may check out software for a scheduled period of time, not to exceed one academic quarter, for office use. All materials from the collection must remain in the building and available for recall when needed in the lab. Faculty may also request certain packages be placed on reserve in the library for a limited amount of time.

Conclusion

The IBM Microcomputer Lab at Raymond Walters College has been in operation for over two years. Since its opening, the hardware has been upgraded to accommodate the specialized needs of faculty. Modems have been installed for the online bibliographic instruction and business courses. Color monitors and additional graphics memory were purchased to display sophisticated medical and chemical graphics software. Various printers to create spreadsheets, graphics, and letter-quality publications were also added to the basic hardware configurations. The computer lab now houses one of the most extensive software collections at the University of Cincinnati, amounting to over 150 titles. The programs and applications in the collection include word processing, accounting, database management, graphics, spreadsheets, training modules, and a variety of programming languages and utilities. The lab also maintains a reference collection of computer magazines, books, articles, and supply catalogs for general use by patrons of the lab. Public domain software and demonstration simulations that can be freely copied are also kept in the reference area.

As the various departments of the college begin to integrate computer instruction into their curricula, more and more software is purchased, and upgrades to hardware continue. Eventually, new labs are created for exclusive use by each department. The library's microcomputer lab then serves as a testing ground, a place where the instructors can get their feet wet before changing their teaching styles and before their department spends a large amount of money on computer equipment of its own. In this way, the lab remains accessible to the individual patrons for whom the initial concept was first conceived.

Chapter Four

California Polytechnic State University

Mary Louise Brady, Head

On May 4, 1986, the Robert E. Kennedy Library opened its Curriculum Micro Center with eight microcomputers. In a period of just one year, over 21,000 students, faculty, and staff have used the eight machines plus printers on an almost continuous basis, asking over 4,000 questions regarding their use.

The Robert E. Kennedy Library, an integral part of the California Polytechnic State University, San Luis Obispo, serves a clientele made up of 16,000 students, faculty, and staff, as well as members of the surrounding community. The university is one of nineteen campuses in the California State University System that offers a four-year undergraduate study program with emphasis in the applied technical and professional fields. Its philosophy is, and always has been, "learn by doing," and that is exactly what one department in the library has been doing in the way of personal computers. The Curriculum Micro Center (CMC) is located on the second floor of the library in the Learning Resources and Curriculum Department. The center is open during the fall, winter, and spring quarters for a total of 89.5 hours per week, and 63.5 hours per week during summer quarter. It is equipped with eight microcomputers, five printers, and a videodisc player connected to an Apple IIe. There are two Apple IIes, two Macintoshes (512K Enhanced), two IBM PCs, one Hewlett-Packard Vectra, and one Hewlett-Packard 150 II. An Apple IIe and a Macintosh are interfaced with ImageWriter I and II printers. A Televideo letter-quality printer is connected to the second Apple IIe, and an Epson FX-85 printer is connected to an IBM PC. The rest of the equipment—one Macintosh, an IBM PC, the H-P Vectra, and the H-P 150—are all cabled to an Hewlett-Packard LaserJet Plus letter-quality printer.

Planning

The decision was made to locate the CMC in the Learning Resources and Curriculum Department (L R & C) of the library, since that department already housed all of the audiovisual equipment used by library patrons. The department also worked closely with the faculty and students of the Education Department, and provided the impetus for getting the center started.

The center grew out of a recognition that the library had to offer more support for the teaching and research functions of the university in the area of computer-assisted instruction and computer-based education. This became even more apparent when, in 1985, the Education Department offered a new master of arts degree in education with a specialization in computer-based education. The new degree was designed to prepare teachers to develop and use computer programs for classroom instruction. In support of this program and others being developed on campus, a proposal was submitted by the library's L R & C staff to the campus administration for a special project allocation to be taken from the general fund.

On September 13, 1985, it was announced that the library would receive $22,594 to assist in the establishment of a microcomputer center with the understanding that the hardware procured would be able to support a wide variety of computer-assisted instruction/computer-based education products. The center would also be able to support a variety of software packages used to produce such products. The CMC would be open to all campus personnel, and would be maintained and staffed by the library. The library would also undertake to incorporate any recent technological advances occurring in the CAI/CBE field, such as integration of microcomputers and laser disc innovations.

The concept of the center was strongly supported by many groups on campus, among them the microcomputer development committee, computer services, and many of the faculty. Before purchasing the equipment, a survey was made of faculty members who were either heavy microcomputer users or were involved with microcomputer development to determine which computers would best serve the needs of the campus. Based on the information gained, and the library's own study, four basic computer brands were purchased: the Apple IIe, the Macintosh, the IBM, and the Hewlett-Packard.

In the year that the center has been in operation, the only computer that has failed to draw its share of the crowd is the H-P 150. However, more and more students are beginning to use it, since it is a powerful machine and they can find an open time slot on it frequently. Statistics show that of all the computers, the Macintosh with the ImageWriter II printer has proven to be the most popular, closely followed by the IBM PC with the Epson FX-85 printer.

After determining which equipment would be purchased, the library then worked closely with the campus bookstore computer division to determine what additional equipment would be needed to make the center functional. Plant operations was requested to augment the power supply in the room where the equipment would be located, furniture was surveyed in the library to see what could be used in the way of computer stations, and several computer students were hired to help get the equipment up and running. A technician from computer services came in at the end to check on all of the work and to finalize the cabling of all the equipment.

Policies

Human nature being what it is, especially when one is dealing with college students, policies were drawn up and then revised several times concerning the actual operation and use of the center. The final draft of "Rules and Regulations" was drawn up on February 2, 1987, and consisted of nine statements:

Figure 10. The Curriculum Micro Center at Kennedy Library

1. In signing for time on the computers, persons agree to abide by all copyright rules. The unauthorized copying or use of software is a violation of the copyright law and subject to the penalties provided by law. Persons observed violating the copyright rules will not be permitted to use the center, and will be reported to the proper university authorities.

2. Persons who are not familiar with how to operate a computer or a printer should be aware that assistance is available only at certain scheduled times of the day. Those who operate a computer incorrectly will be charged for the assessed damage to either the computer itself or the software program used.

3. Persons possessing a valid Cal Poly ID card may sign for a one- or two-hour block of time. No one will be allowed to operate any computer without a valid Cal Poly ID. There will be NO exceptions. In order to avoid a machine being monopolized by one person for an entire day, a person may sign for a two-hour block of time with no more than two nonconsecutive two-hour blocks per day. (Maximum: four hours daily use) Persons may sign up for time in advance. Phone reservations are not accepted.

4. Persons reserving time on the computers must arrive no later than ten minutes after the hour or lose their assigned time.

5. Persons using the computers must provide their own initialized diskettes. The library does circulate computer programs for the various computer models, and users may check these out for use in the room for a two-hour period of time. The user should be familiar with a program before attempting to run it, or be held accountable for any program returned damaged.

6. A fee will be charged for use of the letter-quality printers to cover maintenance costs of those printers.

7. No food or drink is allowed. Library rules pertaining to noise will be maintained.

8. All power is shut down fifteen minutes before closing time. All computer work must be finished or saved by then. There will be NO exceptions!!!

9. The library reserves the right to refuse service to any user.

The rules on the whole are being observed by the users. However, the library did have to reinforce some of the rules with additional warnings, especially the one regarding unauthorized copying of software. To emphasize that the library was serious about condemning unauthorized copying, additional signs were placed in the carrels with a strongly worded message threatening dire consequences. The L R & C staff made arrangements with both the library director and the associate dean of student affairs to deal with students found abusing this rule.

The second policy, regarding people with little or no experience, helped us when students would come to the desk and want to "use a word processor." The litany would go as follows:

"Which computer do you wish to use?"
"Any that does word processing."
"What program do you intend to use?"
"I just need to type a paper."
"Yes, we know, but what program have you used before, do you have a formatted disk, have you ever used a computer before???"

The conversation would continue until one had either convinced the student that perhaps he or she really did want to type the paper on a typewriter, or else to come in when a tutor was available who could get the student started on a simple word-processing program.

Policy number three brought out the greatest creativity on the part of students trying to beat the two-hour and four-hour limit. Many of them could be future lawyers.

Policy number four was a necessity, since many students would sign for a time and then never appear. Saying that the machine became free after the first ten minutes allowed the staff to permit another student to use it and not have a computer sit idle for an hour or two. It also helped to relieve the tension felt by both students and staff.

The rest of the policies are really just a few housekeeping rules. Staff found that students using the laser printer were not concerned about the number of copies they made of their draft or final reports, and so the library initiated a small charge of $1.50 an hour to cover replacement costs of paper and the laser cartridges.

To encourage students to leave on time at closing, it was necessary to warn them that all power would be shut down fifteen minutes before closing in order to be able to clear the library within a reasonable time. Student assistants were staying later and later at night in order to clear the library.

The last policy was put in so that if a patron was found abusing the privilege of using the center, staff would be able to refuse them in the future. The library has yet to find anyone falling into this category.

As students found new ways to get around the various rules, the staff met the challenge with appropriate changes in wording. So far, the staff has stayed ahead.

Staffing

The center is primarily served by the learning resources and curriculum staff composed of three librarians, three library assistants, one clerical assistant, and seventy-two hours of student assistant time. The general supervision of the center is under the head of L R & C.

Each full-time staff member has taken miniclasses dealing with the use of each of the computers, plus various types of software. None of them, however, is expert enough to answer all of the questions that have been or will be asked. In addition to the department's normal reference questions, over 4,000 questions have been logged regarding the use of the computers and/or software. The staff found that no matter how hard they might try, there was no way that they would be able to answer even one-third of the questions without help. Thus was added to the department the computer tutor, a student versed in the use of one or more of the computers, and the more popular software that went with the appropriate equipment.

The students have proven to be excellent tutors. To keep track of the more difficult questions, and to help staff members not familiar with particular computer problems, difficult questions or problems were logged in a notebook with the appropriate answers for all to see and read. This has helped to ease the burden of those caught without a computer tutor on hand, especially at low-usage hours or on weekends.

Software

When the department first got into the computer business with the purchase of an Apple IIe, the collection of software was restricted to that put out for the Apple. With the purchase of additional computers, the decision was made to purchase at least one word processor, spreadsheet, and database manager for each computer.

This, on the whole, has worked well for the users who may borrow a program for use on the computer for two hours. Such a policy also prevents the department from violating any copyright rule. A given program can be used only by one patron on one machine at any given time, unless the library has two copies of the program. Another safeguard that the library implements is the typing of the following rider on the order form itself: "Vendor understands, acknowledges, and agrees that CSU operates a lending Library which regularly lends educational materials, including computer software, to faculty, students, and other patrons." Only one vendor ever cancelled an order after receiving this notice on the purchase form.

A more formal selection policy was developed to cover more than just the software used in the computer center. The statement reads as follows:

> A representative collection of both general application and education software is maintained by the L R & C Department in support of the instructional programs of the University.
>
> Selection of software will be based on the following objectives: to provide a model collection of commercial and teacher-made software for use by faculty and students in conjunction with the curricula program of the University; to provide experience in the utilization and selection of microcomputer software in teacher education, and to select software that is compatible with the computer equipment available in the Library.
>
> Public domain software will be obtained only on a limited basis, and then only if applicable as "systems software" or if it possesses exceptional merit in its own right. A back-up copy will be made, when permissible, for archival purposes only.

Funding

As mentioned earlier, the Curriculum Micro Center was initially funded from a special project allocation taken from the University's General Fund. Ongoing costs, such as maintenance, upgrades, new equipment, software, etc., were absorbed by the library's own budget mechanism. The heaviest expense was the hiring of computer tutors or student assistants to work in the center. Even though they were paid the base rate their salaries added up to several thousand dollars a year.

Maintenance on equipment during the first year has been minimal, but purchase of paper, ribbons, and cartridges has proven expensive for the library.

Funding for computer software was taken from the library's audio-visual software budget, and because computer software is expensive, it made quite a dent in that budget. However, since the first-year funds were spent establishing a basic collection of useful as well as outstanding programs, this expense should not be as great in the coming year. A major decision that will have to be made will be whether to upgrade a program every time a new upgrade appears on the market. The decision to upgrade will be based on how well the new program performs and what reviewers have said about it.

Pros and Cons of CMC

Despite the fact that the library staff feels a bit numb after a year of managing an extremely active computer center, the staff, in general, is willing to continue the operation of the center, but with the understanding that the focus of the center will revert to its original objective.

When the center was first started, it was to be a model library computer center where faculty and students could come and learn about new software and equipment, test programs out on the various computers, look at programs that instructors had assigned for class review, and, in general, utilize the material in the center for their studies as they would any other form of media in the library.

What the center quickly became, however, was another computer lab for students doing resumes, reports, and word processing while utilizing the available laser printer. Many of the users had their own software, so needed only the use of the computers in the center. Because there was not another location on campus having a similar open lab with the same number of hours as provided by the library, or the use of a laser printer, the library felt obligated to continue to support the needs of the students until the campus could find them another computer lab.

A survey was done by the L R & C reference librarian to establish a profile on the type of student who was using the CMC. The results showed:

Class Level : Senior
Major-Dept: School of Engineering (3:1)
Freq of Use: Weekly
Time of Use: No clear pattern
Type of Use: Class assignment (2:1)

Equip Used: Micro with printer
Software: Personally owned (2:1)
Assistance: Computer tutors
Comments: Need more knowledgeable staff, especially at night, need more computers, especially Macs.

In the summer quarter of 1987, a new computer lab, sponsored by the computer services department, was opened to provide just such a general service to students. The library's center will now be able to return to its original purpose of being a model library microcomputer center, and restrict the use of word processing to those previewing software or studying a new program. The laser printer will also be withdrawn from general student use, and reserved for library projects.

Computer Lab versus the Department

The CMC has had a tremendous effect on the L R & C Department. The department head's time has been spent more and more on maintaining the computer center rather than the department. Problems have developed due to the center's high use that have required immediate answers to keep patrons happy. Costs have risen, requiring constant monitoring of the budget to ensure that the L R & C Department did not suffer from having the center.

Staff members have been overburdened with additional duties, and have been obliged to take on new roles that required more training on their part to meet the increased needs of the patrons. The reference librarian has experienced a large increase in the area of reference questions pertaining to the use of the computers, the printers, and the requests for different computer programs to meet various needs of the user. This, in turn, has created a need for an assortment of pathfinders, guides, and software lists to be developed that would assist the user in making intelligent decisions as to finding and using the right software. Cataloging personnel have had the added responsibility of the cataloging and processing software, testing the programs, making the archive copies, and ensuring that all original cataloging conformed to the standards put forth in AACR2 and the Online Computer Library Center (OCLC).

In itself, the Curriculum Micro Center has not been a problem. The only real problem was that it was being managed by a staff that already had a major department to operate, and who have had to make time to run an operation that called for major computer skills that they really were not required to have. What

CALIFORNIA POLYTECHNIC STATE UNIVERSITY LIBRARY
San Luis Obispo, Ca.

MICRO-COMPUTER USE SURVEY

To help the Learning Resources and Curriculum Department in its efforts to provide quality service to users of the Curriculm Micro Center, we would appreciate your honest responses to the following questions. The survey will only take a few minutes. All responses will be treated confidentially.

CLASS LEVEL:

____ Freshman	____ Faculty Member
____ Sophomore	____ Staff Member
____ Junior	____ Library Employee
____ Senior	____ Library Associate
____ Graduate Student	

MAJOR/DEPT _____

FREQUENCY OF USE:
____ Daily
____ Once/Week
____ Monthly
____ Other (Please Specify) _____

TIME OF USE:
____ Morning (M-F)
____ Afternoon (M-F)
____ Evening (M-F)
____ Saturday
____ Sunday

TYPE OF USE:
____ Class Assignment (Reports, papers, etc.)
____ Software Assignment
____ Resume
____ Senior Project
____ Other (Please Specify) _____

EQUIPMENT USED:
____ Microcomputer Only
____ Microcomputer with Dot Matrix Printer
____ Microcomputer with Letter Quality Printer

(OVER)

Figure 11. Survey form used in the Micro Center

SEE FRONT PAGE

SOFTWARE USED:

_____ **Personally owned**
_____ **Library owned**

ASKED ASSISTANCE FROM:

_____ **Student Computer Assistant**
_____ **Library Staff Member**
_____ **A Fellow Student**
_____ **Other (Please Specify)** _____

COMMENTS/SUGGESTIONS:

**THANK YOU FOR YOUR ASSISTANCE IN COMPLETING THIS SURVEY.
PLEASE LEAVE IT IN THE WIRE BASKET ON THE ATTENDANT'S DESK
10/86 W.W.**

Figure 12. Survey form continued

probably saved the center, and helped to make it the sudden success that it was, was the fact that the learning resources and curriculum department staff have always been in the forefront of new technology in the area of audio-visual equipment, and the individual staff members were willing to learn and experiment with this newest technology that had been added to their domain.

The center's biggest enemy has been time or the lack of it. With computer scheduling, helping with software problems and equipment, and guiding the novice in using a computer for the first time, there has not been enough time in the day to fully complete a project. The hiring of more computer tutors helped a great deal, and having the understanding and backing of the library director also went a long way in making the center work.

The staff looks forward to a new year and a new beginning, and the challenges that will arise as they explore new programs, equipment, and technology.

Chapter Five

Rhode Island College

Maureen T. Lapan, Director

Rhode Island College, located on the boundary between Rhode Island's capital city, Providence, and the town of North Providence, is a four-year general purpose college serving both graduate and undergraduate students. One of three state-supported institutions of higher education in Rhode Island, its president and academic officers are responsible to the Board of Governors, which oversees Rhode Island higher education.

Since its founding as the Rhode Island Institute for Instruction by Henry Barnard in the 1840s, its growth has paralleled that of teacher education in the United States as it emerged as a four-year-degree granting college of education, and presently, a college housing a faculty of arts and sciences, a school of social work, a school of education and human development, and a school of continuing education and community service. It has moved from an institution primarily devoted to teacher education to a college with a diverse enrollment. Approximately 8,500 undergraduate students and graduate students are enrolled in the college.

The Curriculum Resources Center at Rhode Island College is a unit of the School of Education and Human Development, serving preservice and inservice teachers and administrators in Rhode Island as well as educators in southeastern Massachusetts and eastern Connecticut. The center provides its patrons access to subject areas at all levels. Included in the collection are subject areas found in elementary and secondary schools in the region as well as those which, it is anticipated, seem likely to be included in school curricula in the near future.

The Microcomputer Center

Seeking to maintain its position as a repository of up-to-date material as well as its function as a catalyst for the development of new and extended instructional programs, the Curriculum Resources Center acquired its first microcomputer, a Bell and Howell Apple, during the spring of 1982. It also purchased a few pieces of software with which to demonstrate the potential of the programs for instruction in elementary and secondary schools.

The acquisition of the first microcomputer was viewed as but the initial step toward the establishment of a microcomputer study center that would enable center patrons to examine a range of instructional programs intended for use in elementary and secondary school classrooms. Unlike the general policy governing the use of instructional material at the Curriculum Resources Center at that time, software from the center's collection could be borrowed on a short-term basis by college faculty only. The bulk of the material in the center collection is available to patrons on a two-week loan basis.

The academic year 1982–83 served as a bench mark for a rapid growth of interest in the instructional and administrative use of microcomputers across the Rhode Island College campus, as well as a growing sense of the need to respond to the developments relating to the instructional use of software by the staff of the Curriculum Resources Center and the faculty of the School of Education and Human Development.

As a result of the interest engendered by the initial microcomputer installation in the Curriculum Resources Center as well as faculty members in the School of Education interested in the instructional implications of microcomputers especially in the area of reading instruction, the dean of the school assisted the Curriculum Resources Center in the acquisition of eleven Apple microcomputers to be used to acquaint faculty and students with instructional applications and to create a demonstration component in the Curriculum Resources Center.

Site Selection and Hardware

It was at this juncture, then, that the decision was made to use a classroom in the Curriculum Resources Center as a microcomputer demonstration facility. It would be compatible with the general goals and functioning of the center and would also provide School of Education faculty and students access to direct contact with hardware and software used in elementary and secondary schools. Likewise, this facility would stimulate interest among elementary and secondary school personnel in this growing area. Apple computers were selected for the facility because a study of the types of hardware in local school systems revealed the Apple computer to be the brand of hardware most frequently purchased by school systems at that time.

Microcomputer Center Activities

What follows is a sampling of the activities engaged in by Rhode Island College faculty and students as well as elementary and secondary school teachers and students with access to the facility:

1. Training classes for School of Education faculty—Introduction to Microcomputers. The classes were taught by college faculty already possessing that expertise.

2. Word-processing training classes for School of Education faculty.

3. In-service classes for teachers and administrators and State Department of Education personnel—Introduction to Microcomputers. Taught by Rhode Island College faculty.

4. Henry Barnard Computer Club—thirty-nine sessions. The club consisted of elementary school students enrolled in the campus laboratory school and their faculty adviser.

5. Mt. Pleasant High School Computer Club—eighteen sessions. The club consisted of secondary school students enrolled at a nearby city high school and their adviser.

6. Instruction for Henry Barnard School students enrolled at the campus laboratory school.

7. Conference groups—Orientation to Microcomputers.

8. Preservice instruction for Rhode Island College undergraduates.

In addition to these activities, which required reservation of the demonstration room for groups of students and faculty, the facility was very heavily used by faculty, students, and public school teachers for the purpose of reviewing software and developing their own computing skills.

Hardware and Software Acquisitions

It should be noted that purchases of capital items and instructional materials—i.e., software—are made through state funds supplied through the regular college budget. From time to time, gifts of instructional materials are given to the center by individuals as well as materials' publishers. For example, the historical textbook collection was developed through gifts of interested individuals; the Reavis Collection through contributions of Kappa Delta Phi; and the Space-Earth Science Collection in cooperation with NASA and the Teacher in Space Program.

Given these precedents, the director of the center contacted all the major vendors of microcomputers requesting long-term deposits of hardware and software in the demonstration center so that users of the facility would have access to software other than that which is Apple compatible. Atari deposited two computers and seven software programs in the demonstration room. Commodore also made a deposit of three computers and appropriate software in the facility prior to June 1, 1983.

Publications

Throughout the years of its operation, the Curriculum Resources Center has developed a modest publications program, which serves the purpose of informing the center's various constituencies about the instructional materials available through the center. The center, therefore, publishes acquisitions lists, annotated bibliographies in areas of special interests, and newsletters.

The first Annotated Bibliography of Microcomputer Instructional Materials in the Curriculum Resources Center compiled by a center graduate assistant was published and distributed to the college community and to all public and private schools in the state in the spring of 1983. The bibliography included the fifty items of new software acquired during the 1982–83 academic year, representing such subjects as elementary and secondary school mathematics, music, physical education, elementary and secondary science, sex and family life, word processing, and items relating to microcomputer instruction.

In addition, the center developed a traditional textbook collection dealing with computer language, programming, use of microcomputers, and a multimedia collection, primarily slides, audiotapes, and filmstrips dealing with similar topics.

Policies

As interest in the educational applications of microcomputers increased in Rhode Island and nationwide, the demonstration room began to feel the weight of conflicting pressures for uses which were not compatible with the mission of the Curriculum Resources Center. Therefore, at the behest of the center's director, the dean of the School of Education appointed a seven-member advisory committee chaired by the director of the center.

This committee, charged with providing advice to the dean regarding the development of instruction in microcomputers and the development of the demonstration facility, met regularly throughout the academic year. In April, the committee submitted a proposal to the dean for the expansion of activity relating to microcomputers in the school, both that of the demonstration center and of the integration of the technology into teacher education programs.

The period 1983–84 was transitional in the development of the demonstration room. It was a time of increasing demands on the microcomputer facility by the Rhode Island State Department of Education personnel, public and private school teachers, interested members of the public, and college faculty and students. Many requests came to center personnel for group instruction in the use of microcomputers, individual consultations, and requests for the off-campus use of software owned by the center. The requests for service far exceeded the capacity of the existing center staff as well as its resources for materials acquisitions. Furthermore, serious concern developed relating to the potential copyright abuse of commercially developed software. The existing resources of the center could not fulfill the demands imposed upon it by concerned educators.

Funding

J. Joseph Garrahy, the 1984 incumbent governor of Rhode Island, proposed the "Governor's High Tech Initiative," which was an attempt to stimulate the sagging economy of the state by attracting to Rhode Island high-tech companies. He proposed the development in the state of a work force competent in the area of technology to staff the sought-out companies. His proposal included the purchase of microcomputers for all school systems in the state for use at both the elementary and secondary levels. Further, the proposal included the provision of workshops for teachers to develop and upgrade their skills relating to the use of computers. Institutions of higher education were also included under the proposal so that the Curriculum Resources Center was the recipient of $30,000 over a two-year period for the purchase of instructional software packages.

The increasing attention focused on the use of microcomputers in elementary and secondary schools was reflected in the increased activity generated in the center's demonstration room. The facility was used by classes in the School of Education and Human Development, individual students, faculty, and representatives of school systems who wished to review center materials, as well as many individuals who worked on their own computer programs. Further, the center was designated as a materials depository for teacher trainers on computers for state workshops. The software collection increased by 111 items and encompassed all elementary and secondary school teaching areas. The purchasing of the software under the governor's program was initiated in 1983–84; however, the bulk of the material was not acquired until the following academic year.

Pressures were so great on the demonstration room that, at the suggestion of the advisory committee, a second center in Horace Mann Hall was created for the purpose of providing a classroom with an IBM and Apple installation for instruction, as well as for students who wished to work independently. The development of the facility freed the demonstration room to fulfill its function as originally intended—that of providing center users an opportunity to examine instructional materials used in Rhode Island and elsewhere—rather than as a classroom facility. During the 1983–84 academic year, the demonstration room acquired software and equipment representing a variety of microcomputer systems—IBM PC, IBM PCjr, Apple II, Macintosh, Atari (donated by the company), TRS-80, and Commodore—as computers of these types were acquired by elementary and secondary schools.

A center graduate assistant particularly competent in the area of microcomputer instruction assumed responsibility for monitoring activities in the demonstration room as well as the production of a new software bibliography during this academic year. The financial support provided through the governor's program, the relocation of classroom activities from the demonstration room to the newly organized instructional center, and the assignment of a college faculty member to the position of part-time demonstration room consultant determined the mode of further development for the demonstration facility.

Funding for the demonstration room remains a part of the overall budget of the Curriculum Resources Center. Capital expenditures are funded through the budget of the dean of the School of Education and Human Development. Support for the part-time faculty consultant is provided by off-loading the faculty member from his usual full-time teaching assignment in the Department of Psychology. Graduate assistants with expertise and special interest in the area of microcomputers are also assigned to assist with the development of the facility.

Software Selection

As is the case with all Curriculum Resources Center acquisitions, the identification and purchase of instructional material and hardware is the responsibility of the center's director. In matters relating to the purchase of equipment, the director maintains contact with elementary and secondary school personnel and members of the State Department of Education to keep on top of developments and future trends in the school. A serious effort is made to keep the center collection reflective of that which is used in area schools as well as nationwide trends and concerns. Further, the technological expertise of the faculty and staff who serve on the Microcomputer Advisory Committee is a major source of input for decision making.

The advice of the members of the committee, faculty who provide instruction in the educational applications of microcomputers, and reviews in professional and computer journals and newsletters provide a source of information for the purchase of software.

Accomplishments

During the first year the faculty consultant was assigned to the center (1984–85), the following tasks were accomplished:

1. Development and maintenance of a database filing system of commercial software showing title, access number, computer, publisher, subject, level, type of program, storage location, and price. The system has gone through several revisions and has been moved from PFS:file to dBase III. The database now has 450 records.

2. Using the database; periodically updating the alphabetical and numerical lists used at the reference desk to locate software.

3. Development of a similar database of public domain software for the Apple computer using PC-File, a shareware filing system. This database now has 950 records.

4. Development of computer literacy skills on the IBM PC with student employees and staff.

5. Production of two issues of the newsletter *Software Resources* for distribution to all public and private elementary and secondary schools in the state as well as at the Rhode Island College campus.

6. Development of a mailing list file using PC-File containing the names and addresses of individuals not ordinarily available through the Publications Office. This list will be used to prepare mailing labels for *Software Resources*.

7. Consultant to faculty and students at the college, and teachers and administrators in local school systems on courseware and other software applications.

8. Installation of software on particular computer models and testing of the software.

9. Designing, producing, and installing a key-activated power switch for the computers in the demonstration room so that the computers cannot be used unless the person checks out a key.

This list of accomplishments in one academic year on a part-time basis indicates the level of accomplishment that can be achieved when a faculty member is free to devote a portion of his or her time to one task exclusively.

During 1984–85, 276 new software items were acquired and incorporated into the center collection. In addition to the increase in the number of items in the collection as well as the range of subject areas treated, the impact of the state-wide distribution of bibliographies and *Software Resources* increased activities in the demonstration room. Approximately 2,000 software items were reviewed in the center by approximately 1,500 center users.

Subsequent years have witnessed the continued growth in both the acquisition of hardware and software as well as the range and number of individuals who use the demonstration room.

Continued Funding

The Rhode Island system of higher education has experienced serious budget reductions in the face of continuing price increases for software and equipment. Keeping an adequate supply of paper and ribbons for printers and disks presents serious problems as does funding for the maintenance of equipment. Although these items are small when seen in the context of large institutional budgets, lack of access to routine supply-and-maintenance funds has proved to be a source of anxiety for many and has resulted in the collapse of some technical services.

In addition, the demonstration room facility strives to represent the best and most recently developed hardware and software available for microcomputer instruction. Such a policy commits the Curriculum Resources Center to continuously revising and developing its collection so that it will be congruent with the most recent technological developments.

SOFTWARE RESOURCES, Vol 1, No. 2, Page 4

PIANO - user creates musical compositons on the computer, that can involve as much as two octaves of notes, sharps and flats, and notes of differing lengths. The compositon can be played at any point, saved on disk, and printed. ($18.00)

LEROY'S CLIFF HANGER - a word oriented game similar to hamgman. The program contains 120 words broken into three levels of difficulty. Users may play against the computer or against each other. ($16.00)

LEROY GOES NETWORK - teacher can create word lists up to 100 words long, and store them on disk or tape. The words may have hints included with them. This program functions in a way similar to LEROY'S CLIFF HANGER. It can be used to help students review word lists and develop skills in areas such as foreign language translation. ($32.00)

FAST FOOD MATH - a how to handle money program for grades 2 through 9. The program simulates food purchases in a fast-food resturaunt, with one student acting as cashier and the others as customers. ($26.00)

TEN BY TEN - a graphics and sound oriented program designed to help pre-school children with the skill of counting. ($10.00)

MATCHMAKER - a game designed to help pre-schoolers develop skill in size and shape differentiation and letter recognition. ($12.00)

MISSLE MATH - provides practice in addition skills. The student is presented with addition problems and must respond with correct answer before a missle hits a city or a shield. ($26.00)

YOUNG WRITER'S NOTE PAD I - a menu driven wordprocessing program with full upper- and lowercase letters. A document can hold 11 screens of text, with each screen containing a maximum of 128 characters. ($22.00)

We understand that MESA will be releasing three additional programs soon, SUBMARINE SUBTRACTION, DIVER ADDITION, and THE WIZARD'S MATH BOARD. All of the programs will be available for you to tryout in our Software Demonstration Room, but you will not be allowed to make copies of them. Copies of the programs may be ordered directly from Middletown Educational Software Association, William Seiple, Director, Middletown High School, Valley Road, Middletown, R.I. 02840.

PAWTUCKET SCHOOL DEPARTMENT'S SOFTWARE CONTRIBUTION

We would like to express our thanks to Bob Reynolds and Roger Landry for providing us with copies of the TRS-80 programs published in CLOAD magazine from September 1979 through April 1984 and two disks of SOFTSWAP programs. All of these programs are being added to our public domain collection and will be available to view and to copy onto your own disks.

Figure 13. A representative page from Software Resources

Given the existing budget constraints, planning for acquisitions often is not made on the long-range and orderly basis that one would hope for, but rather on a short-term, irregular basis in response to the most pressing need. This dilemma grows out of the higher education base on which the facility depends as well as on the sporadic influx of funds through grants and gifts.

Current Holdings

Despite the constraints previously described, the demonstration room currently houses the following pieces of technical equipment:

- Eight printers
- Microcomputers:
  two IBM PCs
  one IBM PCjr
  three Ataris
  one Commodore
  one Amiga
  one Apple II+
  two Apple IIcs
  two TRS-80s
  two Macintoshes
  one Bell & Howell

These acquisitions represent the seriousness of the commitment of the School of Education to the development of the facility. In addition, the collection encompasses 790 pieces of commercially developed software and 1,470 public domain programs.

Policy Statement

The continued publication of *Software Resources* as well as acquisition lists of center instructional materials has drawn a varied clientele to the center. Many of the demonstration room users have sought to borrow software on the same basis as other center materials (two-week loan with no renewal period), to copy material, or to use the demonstration room for word processing or to sharpen game skills.

Problems that have resulted from attempts to abuse copyright restrictions, or to use the facility for purposes incompatible with its purpose, necessitated the development of the policy statement included here. The policy statement was the product of the deliberations of the Microcomputer Advisory Committee.

It appears that some confusion has emerged regarding utilization of the computer facilities housed in Rooms 140 and 182 in Horace Mann Hall. In the hope that inconvenience of students and faculty may be avoided, I have included a description of the function of these facilities....

Microcomputer Software Demonstration Room

The Microcomputer Software Demonstration Room houses microcomputers and software representative of equipment and software used in Rhode Island public and private elementary and secondary schools, as well as school systems in surrounding states. The function of the Demonstration Room is to provide a facility where faculty, college undergraduates and graduate students, as well as Rhode Island educators, may have the opportunity to review and evaluate software relative to its utility in instructional settings. The Demonstration Room is not designed as a general college microcomputer work station.

The microcomputer software housed in the Curriculum Resources Center is part of the Center's non-circulating collection. Its use is ordinarily limited to the Demonstration Room itself. The public domain portion of the software collection may be copied, provided patrons supply their own blank disks. The public domain collection includes software for Apple, Commodore, and TRS-80 computers.

Microcomputer Instructional Center

The Microcomputer Instructional Center houses both Apple and IBM equipment. This facility is used by classes offered by the School of Education and Human Development dealing with the educational uses of microcomputers, as well as the use of microcomputers in administration. This facility may be used as a microcomputer work station when it is not occupied by a class....

Use of software is restricted to the demonstration room. College faculty may borrow software on an overnight basis for the purpose of class demonstration or for use with a practicum group at the laboratory school.

Access and Control

In order to use the microcomputer facility, a patron is required to sign the register at the center's circulation desk showing identification and indicating his/her purpose. The patron is then issued a key which unlocks a small device installed in the power lines of each of the computers, permitting the power to reach the computer. When the patron has completed his/her task, the key is returned to the staff member at the circulation desk, and the patron's identification material is returned.

Because of the fragile nature of the computer disks as well as security concerns, all software is lodged in locked file cabinets behind the circulation desk. All software is listed in book catalogs available in several areas in the center. The items are listed by subject, by publisher, and by brand of microcomputer required. An access number assigned to each item is used by the patron when requesting the software for review. Security measures similar to those used when an operating key is requested are employed.

Additional Equipment

During the 1985–86 academic year, a computer workstation for the blind was installed, the expense borne by the Rhode Island College Office of Special Services. A Mockingboard sound system in an Apple computer is the equipment used in this workstation.

Furthermore, a Hayes modem and a telephone line were installed, linking the center with the electronic bulletin board developed by Professor James Kenney (a faculty member with a specialty in the area of instructional technology), and providing the center with the potential for linkage with Rhode Island schools. Information relating to center acquisitions and public domain software programs will be posted on the bulletin board.

The acquisition of the microcomputers and printers described here necessitated the reorganization of the facility in the fall of 1986. New furnishings designed for microcomputers and printers replaced the large tables to which the microcomputer security devices had been bolted, creating a more hospitable environment.

Curriculum resources centers, because of their mission, house fluid collections reflecting ongoing curriculum innovations, trends, and issues. The changes that took place during the past six years in microcomputer hardware as well as changes in emphasis in the nature of instructional programs fulfilled the expectation of the center staff experienced in dealing with dynamics of the field of instructional material. Thus, the staff responded to the necessity of developing a microcomputer software collection in much the same way it has responded to the development of other special collections within the center—through contacts with college faculty, elementary and secondary school personnel, representatives of the state department of education, professional publications, national reports, and publishers of instructional materials. Continuous appraisal of all collections with an "eye" to the elimination of material no longer relevant to ongoing programs and developing trends is a critical task for center professional staff.

Staffing

The center's staff consists of the following positions: director, librarian, assistant librarian, microcomputer consultant, secretaries, three graduate assistants, and student aides.

The director is primarily responsible for the general administration of the center, with special responsibility for liaison with the college administration, department chairs of the School of Education and Human Development, Rhode Island school systems, and the State Department of Education. The director is responsible for overall collection development and purchasing, including microcomputer equipment and software, as well as supervision of center personnel.

The center's librarian assumes responsibility for the hiring, training, and supervision of student workers, the development of physical facilities, cataloging, and retrieval systems in concert with the director and the assistant librarian, and acquisitions relating to selected phases of collection development.

The assistant librarian is responsible for the cataloging of all center acquisitions, including microcomputer software. She is a member of the microcomputer advisory committee and assistant editor of *Software Resources*.

The microcomputer consultant, whose work at the center deals exclusively with the demonstration room, is assigned to the center on a semester basis. He may be awarded anywhere from four to eight credit hours for work in the center. His assignment includes supervision of the computer facility, recommendations regarding the acquisition of microcomputers and software, training of center staff in basic microcomputer skills, consultation with students, faculty, and other patrons, editing of *Software Resources*, membership on the microcomputer advisory committee, and development and maintenance of the software database.

Graduate assistants participate in all phases of center activities, including supervising student aides, and developing annotated bibliographies and displays. Those graduate assistants with special interest and/or expertise in microcomputers are usually assigned to work with the microcomputer consultant.

Student aides perform basic center operations dealing with circulation of materials, reserves, shelving, and processing of requisitions. Student aides serve patrons seeking admission to the demonstration room. The center could not function without a corps of reliable student aides.

Summary

The commitment of funding and personnel required to develop and maintain a microcomputer facility in an instructional materials center or a library cannot help but cause periodic reappraisal of these projects. In retrospect, it appears that the Curriculum Resources Center had no choice but to develop the facility in order to support teacher education programs in their preparation of new teachers to deal with the types of instructional facilities found in schools and to be knowledgeable about a technology which influences so many aspects of American culture. Further, professional educators have a responsibility to make provisions upgrading the skills of the existing teaching force. Since microcomputers have become part of the school culture, both as instructional and as administrative tools, their incorporation within an instructional materials collection is a requirement.

The question remains, however, as to the degree to which microcomputers will be utilized in schools. Given the present integration of computer operations in all phases of American society, it is unlikely that microcomputers in a school setting can be viewed as a passing fancy.

Accompanying further expansion of their use in instructional settings are the more complex questions of the relation of computer programs to the problems of learning itself and to questions of the appropriateness of the technological/systematic approach to instruction for particular educational goals. Instructional centers and libraries should make media available so that their patrons will not be limited in their choice of information sources.

Chapter Six

A Librarian/Manager's Point of View

Peggy Seiden, Software Manager
Academic Computing, Carnegie-Mellon University

This chapter provides an overview of issues and areas with which concern those considering implementing microcomputer services in academic libraries. It is difficult to provide any sort of coherent guide to the implementation of microcomputer services in academic libraries because the implementation in each case is fairly unique. Although some generalities may apply, it is nearly impossible to say what such services should look like. The approaches to implementing these services are at least as varied as the institutions at which they can be found. Because the individual institution will determine not only the scope and objectives of such services, but also how those services are implemented, the funding sources, and relationships with other campus units, it is imperative that any consideration of microcomputer support services in a library begin with an assessment of the institution.

Institutional Culture

The type of microcomputing support services a university provides is dependent upon its institutional culture. The culture will often also determine the role that the library will play in the overall microcomputer services on a campus. Culture is in part defined by:

- the type of university
- size of the university
- the mission of that university
- the strength of the central authority
- the wealth of the university
- the sources of that wealth

Knowing the parameters of the institutional culture and the computing culture in specific will help the library define its services. By conducting such an overview of institutional politics and mission, the library will know with whom it must negotiate to establish such services, whether such services are feasible, and potential sources of funding. For example, although library services at an institution may be highly centralized, it does not necessarily follow that computing services are equally centralized. At many colleges and universities that have well-integrated library structures, computing power may, to a large extent, lie in the individual academic departments. The library will have to tailor its services towards those whose needs currently are not being met by departments.

At the Spring 1987 EDUCOM Information Technology Seminars on Software Acquisition and Support, Tom West, director of computing and communications for the California State University System, described a matrix of institutional models for planning and managing academic computing services. The key factors in the matrix were the wealth of the institution, the size of the university, and the locus of the decision-making (centralized or decentralized). He was able to derive eight institutional models from this matrix (e.g., small-decentralized-poor, large-centralized-poor, etc.). He then went on to describe who the players are in the planning and implementation of academic computing support services. Typical players are the computer center, departments, colleges, faculty, and the library.

It is interesting to note that he did not give the library a large role in the planning phases, unless the school is small, decision-making is centralized, and there is a fairly low wealth quotient. After implementation, however, he sees the library as a key player in the acquisition and distribution of software in almost all types of institutions. It is evident that the library's traditional role of information collector and information disseminator fits equally well with software.

But what about other services? In what situations do we see libraries today as providers not only of software, but of training and ongoing support for that software? And in what situations do we see libraries taking a more active role in the planning of those services? It is clear that libraries in many universities have the central responsibility for providing microcomputer support services. Why is it that libraries are able to move into this new domain?

Microcomputer services are a curious dilemma for university administrators, librarians, and computer centers. They require a different type of support structure than that traditionally provided by the computer center. Microcomputers have served to expand the base of computer users on campus. The new, applications-oriented user is generally not as technically versed as the old user. The computer center supported a few, select applications for a campus. With the proliferation of microcomputer software to meet the diverse needs of the expanded user community, there is the need to develop new models of service. It should not be surprising to find that a library model provides a coherent structure for such microcomputer services, nor should it be surprising that so many academic libraries have become involved with the provision of these services on their campuses.

The Library, the Computer Center, and the University Administration

The institutional culture will to a large extent determine the relationships between the library and other organizations on campus, although such relationships are often more dependent upon the personalities involved. In fact, true cooperative efforts or mergers of the organizations are very often handshakes between people rather than stated policy. The challenge is often to institutionalize those efforts before the people leave the institution.

Institutionalization allows members of different organizations such as the library and the computer center to work together toward common goals. A real threat to such cooperation is misunderstanding of each other's motives. If the computer center perceives the library as a threat to its "territory," or if the library is left out of key decisions affecting users, feelings of distrust may arise that will be difficult to dispel.

In many cases, the library and computer center will develop a working relationship without appealing to administrators higher up. However, if new sources of continued funding are to be established, the university administration plays a central role by necessity. It should be noted that in some institutions those who provide computing support to the campus may report to the institution's chief financial officer, whereas the library generally reports to the chief academic officer. Nevertheless, cooperative efforts can be established even in these situations, although the impetus will usually be bottom-up rather than top-down.

If the library is entering into negotiations with the computer center, it must first define its priorities and service goals and determine where it can be flexible and where it must stand firm. The library and computer center need to determine who pays for what. Scenarios at different colleges and universities vary widely. Perhaps the computer center will be asked to provide monies for staffing, software, or hardware maintenance, while the library provides space, overall administration, software cataloging, and collection development.

Compromise works at both ends. At Michigan State, when the computer center first approached the library, the terms under which the center wanted the cluster to operate were unacceptable to library staff. A year later, the political climate was different; the computer center revised its terms and negotiations proceeded. It is not only on costs that compromise may be necessary. Configuration of the cluster (how many printers), hours of opening, appropriate uses for the cluster, pay rate for student workers—all these are potential problem points during negotiations.

Cooperation between the library and computer center on a project such as the establishment of microcomputer services can happen at many levels. At the top level, it may be legislated by the university administration. This may happen in smaller schools with highly centralized decision-making. At the middle level, the upper management of the library or the computer center may resolve to jointly implement these services and then relegate the actual implementation to their staffs. At the lower level, the staff may actually form alliances in order to provide better services for their users. These lower-level alliances can happen even when the library chooses to implement microcomputer services independent of any central computing organization. As such services move out of the planning stages and into reality, those with the day-to-day responsibility of maintaining such services may establish informal relationships with their peers in the computer center. These informal relationships allow dialog between these two organizations to extend beyond the planning stages.

Ongoing dialog not only prevents needless replication of services, but also provides the libraries with links to funding sources, university hardware and software discounts, and ways of sharing resources and expertise. Continuing discussions can help determine consistent campus policies for pay rates for student consultants, collection development, or software use; it allows the university to make more advantageous deals with vendors by pooling demand; or it may lead to the development of a single catalog for campus software.

Relationships with the Campus

In the same way, the library needs to establish links with the academic departments and the faculty in those departments. Developing a strong basis of support in academic departments is the best way to win administrative support.

Although the library may already have established liaison programs to departments, the existing library liaison may not be the person to whom the library needs to talk in these instances. It is not unlikely that the person who is responsible for gathering together departmental book orders is the wrong person to represent the department's interests where computing is concerned. Sometimes academic departments may have a computing coordinator or staff who administer departmental computing services. However, if these people are only familiar with the department's research computing needs or office automation needs, or if they simply do not exist, then the library will need to identify the most appropriate person. Often the best people to provide information on what their department's computing needs might be are faculty who have developed software or are using computing in their courses. Such faculty members have often been selected by peers as the departmental computing gurus, and so are already the unofficial chief sources of information about computing in the departments.

At institutions where computing power is decentralized and departmental computing clusters are the norm, there may be opportunities for the library and these departments to form mutually beneficial partnerships for the acquisition of software and for distributed support. The library needs to assess what services the departmental clusters may be providing and to whom. On many campuses, departments differ in the amount of money they can spend for such services. What develops is the "haves and have-nots" inequity in computing access. The library has a great potential to democratize access to computing and support the students and faculty in the poorer departments by identifying the have-nots and targeting support to these groups.

Determining Service Objectives

Undoubtedly the most important consideration for those contemplating the development of some sort of microcomputer service is the purpose of that service. Sometimes a library may not have the luxury of determining the purpose and objectives of a service. It may simply be handed the agenda of a university administrator who wants public access microcomputing on his campus and sees the library as the most logical service point.

Microcomputers often go into libraries because someone other than the librarian wants them. They are brought into the library, but not for any library function or in a programmatic way. Although it can be argued that microcomputers should be used to enhance traditional library strengths (information access and information management), it must also be determined to what extent microcomputers can pave the way for libraries to become involved with nontraditional services. Shouldn't libraries provide tools to access information now being created (database management packages or word-processing packages) or tools for problem solving?

A variety of models of microcomputer services have evolved in libraries over the past few years which clearly are taking libraries in new directions. Some of these services are extensions of existing services. For example, many microcomputer labs are associated with schools of education. Libraries already providing future teachers with access to other audio-visual materials have simply added microcomputers and software to their collections. In many cases this software is limited to K-12 educational programs, and the service focus is to a large extent limited to teacher training. However, other libraries with strong media programs have also expanded those programs to include provision of microcomputer support services and software for the entire campus community.

On some campuses, the public service group in the library has the responsibility for the management of microcomputer facilities. These facilities may contain several types of computers popular in other parts of the campus and offer some combination of general-purpose tools such as word processors, spreadsheets, and courseware. Often, they may serve as reserve rooms for locally developed software.

A less frequently seen model is open-access microcomputers scattered throughout the library. These microcomputers can be used by researchers who need access to library materials and word-processing or database management tools concurrently.

In other colleges and universities, the emphasis may be primarily on the provision of software. As licenses for software evolve toward more liberal terms, it is often permissible for users to take software out of the library. The extent of a library's involvement with software also varies. At schools such as California State University, Chico, and Cal Poly at Pomona, the collection development staff is responsible for buying all the microcomputer software for the campus. On other campuses, the library may choose to build a collection of software that supplements the standard offerings of the public-cluster software acquired by the computer center. The library's collection may be focused on information management or on courseware.

The extent to which a library participates in the planning and implementation of these services varies greatly. On one end, there are microcomputer centers that have been, as it were, imposed from above. These services are basically independent of the library except that they share the space. At the other end are services such as those at the University of Wisconsin–Parkside, where the library established the only public-access microcomputer service on campus. In this instance, the microcomputer service looks very much like academic computing services on other campuses with the library offering a wide range of software, several types of machines, and classes on the use of a variety of software tools.

Funding

What are the long- and short-term costs of such a service? It has been estimated that a university can expect to spend 40 percent of initial hardware costs on maintenance and support. Therefore, even if a library gets its hardware for free, it must, as it were, look the gift horse in the mouth. Many campuses have refused to do so. In fact, one of the leading contributors to campus software piracy was that while campuses were willing to budget enormous sums for hardware, they were not providing any budget for software.

While software and staffing are some of the more obvious expenses to contend with, there are many hidden costs to microcomputer services. Space design and furniture, hardware maintenance, telecommunications (such as links to the mainframe or local area networks), and printing costs require significant commitment of funds. In addition, there are supply costs (disks, paper, toner), security systems, and obsolescence of machines and software.

Where does the library go to fund these new services? Initial funds often come from capital requests. If the computer center and the library are working together on the project, then they will be able to share the start-up costs. The computer center often is in the position to contribute hardware, telecommunications costs, and some standard software packages. Other start-up costs may come from student fees. New York State assesses every student a fee of $25 for computer access. This money is then made available to the state schools to be used for providing microcomputer support.

But over the long run, continuing support needs to come from operational budgets. The library may be able to persuade the administration to support continuing efforts, but a more common way for such projects get funded is reallocation of resources. Software funds are pulled from book funds, staff are pulled from other parts of the library.

Another source of continued funding is the use of capital allocations for software. The costs of packages, and particularly multiple copies of a package, may justify using capital funds for software purchases. Other ways of funding software are through cost control—using public domain software, appealing to vendors for free copies of software, or linking into existing campus discounts. As noted previously, the library should also seek out partnerships with academic departments for hardware upgrades or software. Student consultant salaries can be subsidized by state or federal work-study programs. Pennsylvania has a program of grants for state resident students in technologically related jobs.

Other mechanisms used for funding include cost recovery or charge-back systems. Some libraries charge a per-hour rate for access to computers ($6 for an IBM PC; $8 for an IBM PC/XT). Other schools use charge-back mechanisms similar to what exists in a mainframe environment. Students are allocated a certain amount of money and space for accounts on the mainframe and for printing; any activity beyond that is charged against the student. A more common practice with microcomputers is to charge for printing, either by charging for paper, charging an hourly rate, or installing a vendacard system for use with laser printers. Other schools do not charge but do res'rict access, thereby controlling costs.

Hardware and Cluster Configuration

The decision to acquire a particular type of hardware ideally should be based on policy statements from the university administration as to what equipment they intend to support. Where there is little or no central coordination of hardware on a campus, the library should look at their clientele. A library which serves a graduate science or engineering curriculum will likely have different hardware requirements than one serving a liberal arts undergraduate population. Even where the basic machine type is the same there is a question of peripherals such as graphics cards and printing devices. Where costs are high the library may want to appeal to the academic departments for support of such equipment.

Most manufacturers now have special educational discounts. Both IBM and Apple have worked closely with universities to provide equipment at reasonable cost. Zenith has developed plans in conjunction with schools in Michigan. Compatibles provide realistic, inexpensive alternatives to major manufacturer's machines, but questions of the extent of compatibility and of the solvency of a manufacturer may drive purchasers back to the standard machines.

Even where the university administration or the computer center provides the hardware, the cost of installation is high. For example, at Michigan State, although the Zenith microcomputers the library received were free, the cost of the wiring and room configuration was $35,000 for fifty to sixty machines. Clusters can require special furniture, security, rewiring, and air conditioning in order to be workable. When the cluster is configured, the library must take into account whether it will be used for training. There may be additional needs for video projection or a separate classroom area. The library should determine early on in the planning process whether they will allow the cluster to be used as a classroom. If the room is configured as a training area, it may be difficult for the library to reestablish the space as an open-access lab at a later date.

The library might also want to consider installing a local area network (LAN). In addition to allowing sharing of software, LANs also allow for sharing of printer resources. There are no hard-and-fast rules about the number of machines that should be linked to a printer. If the library can allocate one machine as a print server, the problem with print queues is not as severe. However, if a user must wait until the print queue is clear before continuing on with his or her work, then the library may wish to have more printers available. Desktop publishing software and graphics software are also printer hogs. Consider how the cluster is to be used. One possibility is to establish an express printer and a graphics printer. Another is to have one dot-matrix printer for every two or three machines and a laser printer or letter-quality printer for the cluster for final drafts. In this case, the laser printer could be attached to only one machine, which would be used only for final prints.

One word of caution about LANs. Some software companies will demand that if software is to go on a network, the customer must purchase as many copies as there are central processing units. This can be expensive and is not always reasonable for software that appeals to a fairly small user group. Networks also require additional maintenance and policing to guard against theft of connectors or mischief.

The ghost that haunts us all is not cost so much as obsolescence or trailing-edge technology. Michigan State recently retired their Pet computers, and many of us are now faced with the imminent demise of the IBM PC system. Those planning for microcomputer services must consider that the current technology may be obsolete in two to five years. Furthermore, peripherals and printers have even shorter lives. Nevertheless, no university can afford to sit back until the market stabilizes. There is some hope. In 1983 several major hardware vendors predicted the appearance of a "high function," engineering workstation for under $3,000 by 1986. As of this writing (August 1987), we are still waiting. At least we may have a chance to catch our breath.

Software   Acquisition

Software acquisition involves both collection development and purchase. Both aspects present unique problems that the library is not likely to have experienced before with other media.

Decisions on collection development are often difficult to make for those new to computing. The major question facing the library is whether it will follow a textbook model of acquisition and standardize on a particular set of packages, (e.g., one word processor, one spreadsheet), or whether it will follow the library model and provide a range of packages that meet the diverse needs of a variety of users. In some cases, the library will have little choice. If the library is just one of many public clusters on campus, the software offered may simply be that which the academic computing group on campus has chosen to support.

Ideally, the solution lies somewhere in the middle. Many schools find that for general tool software, word-processing packages, database management packages, spreadsheets, etc., they will standardize on one package in each area. This allows them to provide in-depth support and training in those areas. Then the library can acquire packages to supplement this basic core and meet the needs of specialized user groups.

Although it may prove difficult to decide on which package to standardize, those decisions are often dictated by economic necessity. However, investment in educational software packages (courseware, professional software) should ideally come in response to demand from the campus. Assessing demand is often difficult, although libraries already have a leg up based on a tradition of community needs assessment. Often liaison programs with departments and faculty members are already in place. Furthermore, faculty are used to going to the library and making suggestions for purchases.

Whatever terms the library agrees to set for the purchase of software should be documented in a collection development policy. Such a policy need not be very different from those designed for other media. At California State–Chico, where librarians are responsible for central purchase of software, the staff follows guidelines established for the purchase of other media—no textbooks, laboratory materials, or office supplies. In the best of worlds, evaluation would play a major role in the decision process. However, evaluation of software is time consuming and, ultimately, subjective. If staff time is at a premium, evaluation does not necessarily pay for itself. Furthermore, there is an increasingly large number of publications that perform this service. These publications range from digests of already published reviews to consumer reports-type product comparisons. Journals such as *Choice* and *Booklist* have also begun to carry reviews of software. If possible, the library should subscribe to a core collection of journals such as *InfoWeek* and *MacWorld* in order to keep up with new products and reviews.

Purchase of software presents its own set of difficulties. Whereas book and journal prices are set, an acquisition department may often be called upon to negotiate licenses with software vendors. Although there are many jobbers who handle software, much of it must be acquired directly from the publisher. This puts an increased burden on the acquisitions department, which must either spend time negotiating with publishers or searching through various discount houses to get the best price on software purchases. The purchase of single copies may be troublesome enough, but the problems are compounded when purchasing for a cluster or lab, and negotiating site licenses or multiple-copy discounts. There are no hard-and-fast rules here. Many of the better-known publishers have developed educational marketing programs, whereas others make it known that they are open to suggestions.

Perhaps the greatest area of difficulty is the license agreement. Most microcomputer software comes with a shrink-wrap license. Although the terms in the license may preclude loans of the software by libraries, it is difficult for libraries to know these terms before purchase. Licenses will often sound much more restrictive than the publisher's intent. A library may choose to negotiate new terms with a publisher, and in many cases, publishers are eager to comply. As such activity can be extremely time consuming, many libraries have adopted a policy whereby they include, either on the purchase order or along with it, a statement regarding how the software will be used. Acceptance of the purchase order under those terms is thought to constitute a legal and binding contract. Even if challenged, libraries would be in a strong legal position since the producer or distributor had been put on notice and a written record of the library's intent would exist. Software probably will still arrive with the typically restrictive licensing agreement that needs to be signed in order to ensure warranty rights and support. Some universities, preferring to risk damaged software to litigation, have stipulated that such forms should not be signed. The librarian should confer with university counsel to determine any university-wide policies in this area.

Over the last two years, site licenses and multiple-copy discounts have evolved as a way to provide wider and more inexpensive access to software. True site licenses are rare, in part because vendors have little control over the number of copies made and whether those copies are used off the site. Usually, vendors offer heavy discounts for multiple copies. The vendor frequently will provide one copy of the software and manual and the site administrator has the responsibility of making copies of the software. Additional manuals may be purchased at discount. A few vendors are experimenting with the "golden disk" concept. This type of license allows the university to load software on a mainframe and download that software or otherwise make as many copies as are needed on campus. Other vendors have tried to mimic mainframe licenses with annual fees for a set number of copies. It is increasingly rare for the library to pay retail price for software as more and more pricing options become available.

One option open to libraries, eager to avoid legal hassles and concerned over copyright violations, is collecting public domain software or shareware. When a program is placed in the public domain, the author relinquishes control over that program by not copyrighting it. Users can then freely copy the program or create derivative works. The software may be distributed via user groups, libraries, and electronic bulletin boards. Shareware, or user-supported programs, differs from public domain or freeware in that the author requests donations from users if, after trying the program, they decide to keep it. Some authors are casual about the process, but others may support their programs full time. To encourage payment, some authors ask users to pay a registration fee which then guarantees support, documentation, and updates. The lines between shareware and commercial software are becoming increasingly blurred, although shareware has some advantages for libraries because illegal copying is not an issue.

Cataloging and Circulating Software

As soon as software is received by the library, it should be checked for data integrity. A significant percentage of software does not run and disks can easily be damaged in the mail. The library can make one back-up or archival copy for every piece of software it purchases. Many packages today are copy protected, and although there is software available for copying such disks, it does not always work. Libraries may want to set policies about not purchasing software that cannot be copied. Although ideally a library will want to archive the original disk, this is not always possible. Frequently, producers will require that the master disk (the original) be used as a key to start up the program.

Few libraries circulate their software externally. Most labs function as reserve rooms, where the user can take software only to be used within the microcomputer lab. Although such a policy may cut down on illegal copying and theft, most license laws do not discriminate between internal and external circulation of software. Restricting software to in-house use may create queuing problems as students compete for machines. The library may wish to institute a reservation policy for machines or restrict class use.

As with any other library material, the software should be cataloged. More and more libraries are fully cataloging their software, although lists by title or accession number are still prevalent. However, the usefulness of these types of lists beyond inventory control is open to question. ALA recently issued revised cataloging standards for AACR2, Chapter 9, and recommendations for subject cataloging. As software records increase in OCLC (at the present time there are more than 12,000 MRDF records), cataloging of software will become less burdensome. Nevertheless, the unique qualities of software still create problems for the cataloger, who often has two or three different titles, version numbers, and machine requirements with which to contend.

Staffing

How does one staff a microcomputer service? Ideally, the library should determine program goals and needs and develop a job description(s) to suit those objectives. In most cases, however, libraries do not have the luxury of hiring additional professional or paraprofessional staff to manage the new service. The general pattern seems to be to hire initially from within the professional staff. If the service has developed as part of the media services, then staff is drawn from that department; if the public service staff are responsible, then a reference person may be asked to oversee this new service. Often this person has other responsibilities and is expected to work 50 percent of his or her time on microcomputer support. If use justifies expansion of services, the library may have a good case for additional funding for a full-time position. In a number of libraries, paraprofessionals have been hired to oversee day-to-day operations.

In order to help mitigate the pressure that a new service places on the library as a whole, the service should be integrated into existing library structures wherever possible. When additional staff are not to be hired, it is imperative that other departments such as technical processing be brought in to support the function of the new service. Collection-development librarians should be able to suggest software for purchase as well as other media. Acquisitions and cataloging staff should be trained to deal with software. Although equipment repairs can present some difficulties, those responsible for repair of copiers and audio-visual equipment can often handle routine repairs. Library's system staff can often help with the selection of hardware, telecommunications equipment, and software. The greatest additional burden will be in the area of support for users of the hardware and software.

The most popular way to provide this support is to staff microcomputer services with student assistants. At schools where computer literacy is high, costs of providing this type of staffing are generally low. But where computer skills are still a relatively rare commodity, the library may need to pay higher salaries than those paid to other student assistants in order to attract the more knowledgeable students.

In hiring students, it is critical to pay attention to their public service skills. These skills are equal in importance to technical knowledge. Students who can be gracious even under fire usually gain more respect from their fellow students and from faculty than does a surly computer hacker.

In addition to circulating software and providing basic consulting, students may be responsible for troubleshooting, making back-ups, developing in-house documentation, and performing routine clerical tasks. In certain situations, the library may find it appropriate to hire graduate students to assist with tutoring, faculty advisement, and classroom teaching.

Ongoing Support

Computer users have different expectations for service than most library users. It is often said that computer users want everything and they want it yesterday. By the time a computer user asks for help, he or she is usually extremely frustrated and perhaps at wits' end. Rarely does a reference librarian see that type of patron.

Furthermore, the typical computer user is more naive about computing than in the past. In the days of mainframe computing and time-sharing systems when computer cycles were expensive, the average user was far more sophisticated and knowledgeable about computers than the average microcomputer user is today. The mainframe user knew the language and the technology and had little trouble communicating with the user consultant. Furthermore, the community was small enough that user service organizations had a fairly good acquaintance with their highly specialized needs.

As microcomputers proliferate on campus and as "computer literacy" is required at more and more colleges and universities, novice or infrequent users make up an increasingly large faction on campuses. These users need and often expect a certain level of support and training. What role can the library expect to play in this ongoing training and support?

The library must determine the extent to which it will support the software packages it acquires. The library may choose only to provide the documentation that came with a package; it may choose to provide some support in terms of training the staff on certain packages and development of supplementary documentation; it may choose to provide training for users in certain packages. Usually, the library will provide some combination of the above. If that is the case, then it is incumbent upon the library staff to educate users as to what they may expect from each package. It may be useful to develop some sort of support-level scheme (A–D where A is unsupported and D is full support and classes) and record relevant information on the catalog record.

Because the costs of support are so high, a number of institutions are moving towards a distributed support model. This may mean that someone in the statistics department provides support for statistical software or that someone in the social sciences supports decision-modelling packages. If the library is buying the software upon recommendation or request by faculty, the library may be in a position to bargain for distributed support. At California State University–Chico, faculty are responsible for providing all technical and content support for the software provided by the library.

Another mechanism for distributing support is the establishment of user groups. Although such groups cannot provide immediate support, they can serve as a referral service to experts on certain applications. In the same way, online bulletin boards can be created for the purpose of providing advice to users on hardware and software. Users can submit questions and professional staff can respond publicly so that others benefit from their questions.

If the library is required to train its own staff (if the computer center does not staff the cluster), then the library should try to buy into existing microcomputer support mechanisms on campus. If the computer center has a training program for its cluster assistants, the library should work with the computer center to develop consistent training across the campus. This is especially true where the microcomputer cluster in the library provides similar services and software to other clusters run by the computing center. If there are classes for training in various software packages, the library staff and students who are responsible for the microcomputer services should be encouraged to attend.

It is not my purpose here to discuss whether or not libraries should teach word-processing classes or if instruction in bibliographic or information management is the only activity appropriate to these service centers in libraries. Both these activities are prevalent in existing microcomputer services in libraries. The range of packages and training programs that are appropriate are as individual as the institution. In certain institutions, the library may be the only department with concern in fundamental computer literacy. If such a void needs to be filled, then one cannot say that it is inappropriate for the library to do so.

Although training sessions may be held at any time, the most successful may be those that are integrated into classes—word-processing classes for freshman English, presentation graphics for business classes—in much the same manner as bibliographic instruction classes.

Appropriate Use of Software and Computing

Librarians have found themselves increasingly in the position of responsibility for educating users as to the appropriate use of software and respect for intellectual property. With little case law on the books, libraries and universities are unsure of their liability when it comes to lending software. Copyright law may be murky, but even more confusing are the shrink-wrap licenses. In order to remove themselves from threat of litigation, those responsible for managing microcomputer services must take steps to educate their users as to the appropriate use of software. Steps toward this end include posting signs regarding the copyright law and appropriate penalties near every machine, adding disk labels with warnings, asking users to sign a statement saying they will not copy software, and circulating copy protected disks. Recently, EDUCOM and ADAPSO collaborated on a brochure on appropriate use of software. Librarians may wish to make copies available at service points or in the lobby to have such information distributed to all members of the campus community.

In addition, library staff may find themselves policing clusters. Although it is difficult to police clusters, and impossible to watch for abuse of software that circulates externally, software copiers are often indiscrete. The librarian should actively seek out support from the dean of students for disciplinary action and ensure that abuse of software is perceived by all those concerned on campus as inappropriate behavior. The best way to ensure consistent policy is to lobby for the adoption of a statement in student and faculty handbooks. EDUCOM has developed such a statement which appears in the previously mentioned brochure, and it has already been adopted on numerous campuses.

Conclusion

Academic libraries are involved in a range of activities, all going under the name of public access microcomputer services. What is clear is that, although these services take many forms in different institutions, there is a common commitment to service and access. For that reason, libraries have been successful and gained respect from a new group of users.

Chapter Seven

Bibliography

The following annotated bibliography describes books and articles that will provide additional information about microcomputer labs in academic libraries.

Association of Research Libraries. Microcomputer Software Policies in ARL Libraries, Kit 123. Washington, DC: Association of Research Libraries, 1986.

This SPEC kit reports the results of an ARL survey regarding microcomputer software to which seventy-four libraries responded. Also included are copies of acquisition and collection development policies, use and circulation policies, and institution-wide committee and task force reports. Several of the policies relate to software use in microcomputer centers.

Avalone, Susan. "Public Access to Microcomputers." *Library Journal* 110, no. 8 (1985): 135–36.

This article is a report of a *Library Journal* survey of fifty public and fifty academic libraries regarding their microcomputer hardware and software policies. It includes the titles of popular software and lists some of the more common problems that were reported.

Baldridge, J. Victor, Janine Woodward Roberts, and Terri A. Weiner. *The Campus and the Microcomputer Revolution.* New York: Macmillan, 1984.

This book addresses the concerns of top college administrators regarding the installation and proliferation of microcomputers on campus. Librarians will find that the sections dealing with practical issues and training offer suggestions and guidelines for labs to be established in libraries and other campus locations.

Cimbala, Diane J. "There Goes the Neighborhood!" *Technicalities* 5, no. 6 (1985): 9+.

The experience of setting up and maintaining a microcomputer lab at Augusta College's Reese Library is described in this article. Some of their initial problems with sharing responsibility with the Computer Services Department, using the equipment, software processing, and reservations are discussed. The importance of honoring copyright regulations was impressed upon students when a noncollege user of the microcomputer lab was arrested while at the library and jailed for copyright violations. The microcomputer lab is considered an outstanding success and has brought about an increase in the use of the traditional library services.

Curtis, Howard, ed. *Public Access Microcomputers in Academic Libraries.* Chicago, IL: American Library Association, 1987.

The Mann Library's Microcomputer Center at Cornell University is the subject of this book, written by several members of the library staff. It details how the library has provided microcomputers and a software library that support the information-retrieval functions of the library.

Dewey, Patrick R. *Public Access Microcomputers: A Handbook for Librarians.* White Plains, NY: Knowledge Industry, 1984.

Although Dewey addresses the public access situation in public libraries, this book is an excellent source of information for any librarian considering introducing this service. The information is clear, concise, and to the point. Also included are examples of public access projects, information on electronic bulletin boards, a glossary, and a bibliography.

EBSS Ad Hoc Subcommittee on Microcomputer Issues in Education   Libraries. "Administrator's Checklist of Microcomputer Concerns in Education Libraries." *College & Research Libraries News* 47 (1986): 69–71.

While this article addresses itself to administrators of education libraries, the questions raised are relevant for any academic librarian considering the implementation of a microcomputer service. Topics covered include: needs assessment, administrative concerns, hardware, software, circulation, copyright, and service.

Guskin, Alan E., Carla J. Stoffle, and Barbara E. Baruth. "Library Future Shock: Revolution and the New Role of the Library." *College & Research Libraries* 45 (1984): 177–83.

The authors advocate for the library to become the campus hub of information technology. They maintain this position because librarians have become knowledgeable about computer technology, are people-oriented, and responsive to the information needs of faculty and students. Also, the library provides a nonthreatening environment for microcomputers to be used as educational tools and should be at the center of information exchange and technology on the university campus.

Hall, Hal W. "Microcomputer Centers in Libraries: Staffing Considerations." *Library Software Review* 5 (1986): 341–44.

This article describes the analysis that is needed of the function and services of a library microcomputer lab in order to determine the amount of staffing that will be required. Hall indicates the importance of specifying what level of service will be provided in order to avoid confusion and frustration on the part of both staff and users.

ICCE Policy Statement on Network and Multiple Machine Software. Eugene, OR: University of Oregon, 1983.

This statement issued by The International Council for Computers in Education addresses the responsibilities of educators, vendors, and software developers. Included with the statement is a sample copyright policy for a community college microcomputer lab.

Lytle, Susan S., and Hal W. Hall. "Software, Libraries, and the Copyright Law." *Library Journal* 110, no. 12 (1985): 33–39.

The authors discuss copyright law in relation to microcomputer software used in an academic microcomputer lab. Coping with software licenses and agreements, the need for archival copies, piracy, and illegal copying are some of the issues they have dealt with at Texas A&M University. They recommend that each administrator develop guidelines that will protect producers, patrons, and the library.

Piele, Linda J. "Circulating Microcomputer Software." *Access: Microcomputers in Libraries* 2, no. 4 (1982): 7+.

The planning and decisions that were involved in offering a public access microcomputer service at the library of the University of Wisconsin-Parkside are described in this article. Topics included in the discussion are: objectives, policies and procedures, equipment, the selection, circulation, and processing of software, staff training, and security.

Piele, Linda, Harold Tuckett, and Donna Nicholson. "Microcomputer Labs, Software Collections, and Related Services in Academic Libraries." *Catholic Library World* 57 (1986): 225+.

This article reviews the varying roles that academic libraries and librarians are taking as they become involved with public-access microcomputers. These include the purchase and circulation of software and administering the microcomputer center. A list of specific questions that should be addressed before final decisions are made is included. Some issues referred to are: goals, population, demand, software, hardware, and copyright.

Piele, Linda J., Judith Pryor, and Harold W. Tuckett. "Teaching Microcomputer Literacy: New Roles for Academic Librarians." *College & Research Libraries* 47 (1986): 374–78.

According to the authors, microcomputer labs in academic libraries offer librarians the opportunity to promote both computer and information literacy on the college campus. This article describes the program at the University of Wisconsin–Parkside, in which public service librarians have successfully assumed responsibility for the workshops and seminars offered in the microcomputer lab.

Polly, Jean Armour. *Public Technology: The Library Public Access Computer.* Volume 1 of *Essential Guide to Apple Computers in Libraries.* Westport, CT: Meckler Publishing, 1986.

The information contained in this book is based on a survey of 100 public libraries and the author's experience at the Liverpool (NY) Public Library. Even though this volume's emphasis is on Apple computers available in public libraries, several sections, including those on hardware set-up and software management, will be of interest to academic librarians.

Reed, Mary Hutchings, and Debra Stanek. "Library and Classroom Use of Copyrighted Videotapes and Computer Software." *American Libraries* 17 (1986): A-D.

Written by an ALA attorney, these guidelines address questions frequently asked about the purchase, use, copying, and loaning of software programs by libraries.

Smith, Dana. "The Micro Center Monitor Program." *Small Computers in Libraries* 7, no. 4 (1987): 16-18.

Student employees developed The Micro Center Monitor Program described in this article. The program supports the operation of the public microcomputer facility at Cornell University and is available from the authors. Program features include: supervision of machine use, queuing, software circulation, and statistics.

Snelson, Pamela. "Microcomputer Centers in Academic Libraries." *Small Computers in Libraries.* Part I: vol. 5, no. 6 (1985): 6–9; Part II: vol. 5, no. 7 (1985): 7–9.

These two articles record the responses of Howard Curtis (Cornell University), Dee Dee Pannell (Florida Institute of Technology), and Hal Hall (Texas A&M University) to a series of questions about microcomputer labs that the author addressed to each of the participants. This style makes it possible to easily compare the answers the panel members gave to questions about location, instruction, software collections, and the problems of microcomputer centers.

Snelson, Pamela. "Microcomputers in Academe: Challenges and Opportunities for Libraries." *West Virginia Libraries* 38 (1985): 6–13.
Snelson discusses the proliferation of microcomputers on college campuses and the ways that they can be used in the academic library. The establishment of microcomputer labs is one way that colleges are responding to this microcomputer revolution. Librarians can react passively or actively or they can assume an integrative role using the microcomputer to expand existing library services.

Uppgard, Jeannine. "Public Access Microcomputers in Academic Libraries." *Small Computers in Libraries*. Part I: vol. 7, no. 1 (1987): 28–32; Part II: vol. 7, no. 2 (1987): 10–11.
The results of a survey of forty-five academic libraries that have public access microcomputers are summarized in this two-part article. Some of the topics addressed are brands of microcomputers, location of the equipment, noise, software, and overall management of the facility.

Walsh, David B. "The Circulation of Microcomputer Software in Academic Libraries and Copyright Implications." *The Journal of Academic Librarianship* 10, no. 5 (1984): 262–66.
This article explores the extent of academic library involvement in providing microcomputer hardware and software to their patrons. The results of a survey of 293 community colleges, colleges, and universities are summarized in the article, which also includes a discussion of software copyright problems.

Walton, Robert. *Microcomputers: A Planning Guide for Librarians and Information Professionals*. Phoenix, AZ: Oryx, 1983.
This excellent work contains information relating to all aspects of microcomputer use in libraries. Of specific interest to those working with microcomputers in a lab situation are Chapter 11—"Selecting and Purchasing the Right Microcomputer System" and Chapter 12—"Setting Up the Microcomputer System."

Yeaman, Andrew R. J. "Microcomputer Learning Stations and Student Health and Safety: Planning, Evaluation, and Revision of Physical Arrangements." *Educational Technology* 23, no. 12 (1983): 16–22.
This article suggests using knowledge gained from ergonomics and industry to set up microcomputer learning stations for students that will take into account

considerations of health and comfort. A checklist of questions dealing with equipment, furniture and lighting is included.

Chapter Eight

Directory of Library Installations

The following directory was compiled with the help of librarians who responded to a questionnaire sent to some 200 institutions in the spring of 1987. There certainly are other academic libraries offering public access microcomputer labs and we regret that they are not listed here. It is also important to note that with the constant introduction of new products, the number and type of computers available at each library will certainly change to take advantage of the new technology.

Alabama

COLLEGE:	University of Alabama at Birmingham
	Mervyn H. Sterne Library
	Educational Technology Services
	University Station
	Birmingham, AL 35294
	(205) 934-2379
CONTACT PERSON:	Steven G. Laughlin
	Head, Access Services
MICROCOMPUTERS:	60 IBM PC
SOFTWARE TITLES:	75

Arizona

COLLEGE:	Arizona Western College Library
	P.O. Box 929
	Araby Road
	Yuma, AZ 85364
	(602) 726-1000 x360
CONTACT PERSON:	Eileen Shackelford, Director
MICROCOMPUTERS:	2 Apple IIe, 1 Macintosh, 1 Apple IIGS
SOFTWARE TITLES:	175

COLLEGE:	University of Arizona Music Collection
	115 Music Building

Tucson, AZ 85721
(602) 621-7009
CONTACT PERSON: Dorman H. Smith, Head Music Librarian
MICROCOMPUTERS: 4 Apple IIe
SOFTWARE TITLES: 25

California

COLLEGE: California Polytechnic State University
                    Learning Resources & Curriculum Dept.
                    Robert E. Kennedy Library
                    San Luis Obispo, CA 93407
                    (805) 546-2273
CONTACT PERSON: Mary Louise Brady, Head
                    Learning Resources & Curriculum Dept.
MICROCOMPUTERS: 2 IBM PC, 2 Apple IIe, 2 Macintosh, 1 H-P Vectra
                    45, 1 H-P 150
SOFTWARE TITLES: 286

COLLEGE: California State University–Chico
                    Meriam Library
                    Chico, CA 95929-0295
                    (916) 895-5727
CONTACT PERSON: Bill Post
                    Assistant University Librarian, Collection
MICROCOMPUTERS: 10 Macintosh, 4 Apple IIe, 3 IBM PC
SOFTWARE TITLES: 150

COLLEGE: California State University—Fullerton
                    Curriculum Materials Center
                    POB 4150
                    Fullerton, CA 92634
                    (714) 773-2714
CONTACT PERSON: Mary E. Crimmins
MICROCOMPUTERS: 2 Apple II
SOFTWARE TITLES:

COLLEGE: Saddleback College Library
                    28000 Marguerite Parkway

	Mission Viejo, CA 92692
	(714) 582-4543
CONTACT PERSON:	Steven Tash, Reference Librarian
MICROCOMPUTERS:	3 Apple IIe, 2 IBM PC
SOFTWARE TITLES:	120

COLLEGE:	University of Southern California
	Norris Medical Library
	2003 Zonal Avenue
	Los Angeles, CA 90033
	(213) 224-7231
CONTACT PERSON:	Janis Brown Assoc. Director
	Educational Resources
MICROCOMPUTERS:	30 IBM PC, 5 IBM XT
SOFTWARE TITLES:	100+

COLLEGE:	University of Southern California University Library
	University Park Campus - MC 0182
	Los Angeles, CA 90089
	(213) 743-3455
CONTACT PERSON:	Lee Jaffe, User Services Librarian
MICROCOMPUTERS:	50 IBM PC, 18 Macintosh SE
SOFTWARE TITLES:	N/A

Connecticut

COLLEGE:	Central Connecticut State University
	Burritt Library, Curriculum Lab
	1615 Stanley Street
	New Britain, CT 06050
	(203) 827-7542
CONTACT PERSON:	Dona Ostrander, Curriculum Librarian
MICROCOMPUTERS:	1 Apple
SOFTWARE TITLES:	40+

COLLEGE:	Fairfield University
	Nyselius Library
	North Benson Road

	Fairfield, CT 06430
	(203) 254-4044
CONTACT PERSON:	John McGinty, Associate University Librarian
	Virginia Gray Cramer, Head Media Librarian
MICROCOMPUTERS:	8 Apple IIe, 1 IBM PC XT
SOFTWARE TITLES:	28

COLLEGE:	Western Connecticut State University
	Ruth A. Haas Library
	181 White Street
	Danbury, CT 06810
	(203) 797-4052
CONTACT PERSON:	Martin Warzala
MICROCOMPUTERS:	16 DEC Rainbow, 3 Apple IIe, 4 IBM PC XT
SOFTWARE TITLES:	

COLLEGE:	Yale University
	Sterling Memorial Library
	120 High Street
	New Haven, CT 06520
	(203) 436-8335
CONTACT PERSON:	Frederick Martz
MICROCOMPUTERS:	16 IBM PC, 8 Macintosh
SOFTWARE TITLES:	10

Deleware

COLLEGE:	Widener University–Delaware
	Delaware Campus Library
	POB 7139
	Concord Pike
	Wilmington, DE 19803
	(302) 478-3000
CONTACT PERSON:	Jane E. Hukill
MICROCOMPUTERS:	10 IBM PC
SOFTWARE TITLES:	12

District of Columbia

COLLEGE: George Washington University Medical Center
Himmelfarb Health Sciences Library
2300 Eye Street, NW
Washington, DC 20037
(202) 676-2850

CONTACT PERSON: Elaine Martin, Asst. Dir.
Inform. & Instructional Services

MICROCOMPUTERS: Apple IIe, Macintosh, IBM PC

SOFTWARE TITLES:

COLLEGE: Georgetown University
Law Library
600 New Jersey Ave., NW
Washington, DC 20001
(202) 662-9160

CONTACT PERSON: Gary Bravy, Media Librarian

MICROCOMPUTERS: 10 IBM PC XT, 1 Apple IIe, 1 Macintosh

SOFTWARE TITLES: 11+

Florida

COLLEGE: Chipola Junior College
Learning Resources Center
1200 College Street
Marianna, FL 32446
(904) 526-2761

CONTACT PERSON: Jane Walker

MICROCOMPUTERS: 2 IBM PC, 6 Apple IIe

SOFTWARE TITLES: 50

COLLEGE: Florida International University Athenaeum
Tamiami Campus
Miami, FL 33199
(305) 554-2413

CONTACT PERSON: Ron Martin, Head
Instructional Resource Center

MICROCOMPUTERS: 7 Zenith, 1 Apple IIc, 1 TRS 80

SOFTWARE TITLES: 95

COLLEGE: Florida Keys Community College
                     Smith Learning Resources Center
                     5901 W. Jr. College Road
                     Key West, FL 33040
                     (305) 296-9081
CONTACT PERSON: Maria J. Soule, Librarian
                     Patricia Ryan, Microcomputer Lab Coordinator
MICROCOMPUTERS: 6 Apple IIe
SOFTWARE TITLES: 105

Georgia

COLLEGE: Augusta College
                     Reese Library
                     Augusta, GA 30910
                     (404) 737-1745
CONTACT PERSON: Diane J. Cimbala
                     Assistant Librarian for Support Services
MICROCOMPUTERS: 20 Apple IIe & IIc, 10 IBM PC, 30 Zenith 158
SOFTWARE TITLES:

Hawaii

COLLEGE: West Oahu College
                     University of Hawaii
                     94-063 Ala Ike
                     Pearl City, HI 96782
                     (808) 455-0497
CONTACT PERSON: Rose Myers, Librarian
MICROCOMPUTERS: 1 IBM AT, I IBM XT, 1 IBM PC, 2 Apple IIe
SOFTWARE TITLES: 50

Illinois

COLLEGE: Illinois State University
                        Milner Library
                        Normal, IL 61761
                        (309) 438-7250
CONTACT PERSON: Gary Nardi, Supervisor
MICROCOMPUTERS: 70 Zenith, 5 Apple IIe
SOFTWARE TITLES: 25

COLLEGE: Northwestern University
                        Schaffner Library
                        339 E. Chicago Avenue
                        Chicago, IL 60611
                        (312) 908-8422
CONTACT PERSON: Susan Swords Steffen
MICROCOMPUTERS: 20 Zenith
SOFTWARE TITLES:

COLLEGE: Southern Illinois University
                        Lovejoy Library
                        Audio Visual Services
                        POB 1052
                        Edwardsville, IL 62026
                        (618) 692-3050
CONTACT PERSON: Claudia Davidage Supervisor,
                        A.V.S. Microcomputer Center
MICROCOMPUTERS: 32 Apple IIe, 18 Zenith
SOFTWARE TITLES: 150

COLLEGE: University of Illinois at Urbana-Champaign
                        Commerce Library
                        101 Library, 1408 W. Gregory Drive
                        Urbana, IL 61801
                        (217) 333-3619
CONTACT PERSON: Karen Chapman, Asst. Commerce Librarian
MICROCOMPUTERS: 16 IBM PC
SOFTWARE TITLES: 5

Indiana

COLLEGE: Earlham College
                        Wildman Science Library
                        Richmond, IN 47374
                        (317) 983-1245
CONTACT PERSON: Sara Penhale, Science Librarian
MICROCOMPUTERS: 20 IBM PC, 2 IBM AT
SOFTWARE TITLES: 8

COLLEGE: Purdue University
                        Undergraduate Library
                        Stewart Center
                        W. Lafayette, IN 47907
CONTACT PERSON: Patrick Canganelli
                        Information Systems Specialist
MICROCOMPUTERS: 1 Zenith 148, 3 Apple II+, 6 Commodore 64
SOFTWARE TITLES:

Iowa

COLLEGE: Luther College
                        Preus Library
                        Decorah, IA 52101
                        (319) 387-1166
CONTACT PERSON: Jane Kemp, Circulation-Reference Librarian
MICROCOMPUTERS: 8 Macintosh, 8 Zenith, 3 IBM
SOFTWARE TITLES: 4

COLLEGE: University of Iowa
                        College of Education
                        Learning Resources Center
                        N153 Lindquist Center
                        Iowa City, IA 52242
                        (319) 335-5620
CONTACT PERSON: John Achrazoglou
MICROCOMPUTERS: 25 Apple II, 7 Macintosh, 2 IBM PC, 5 Leading Edge
                        Model D
SOFTWARE TITLES: 400

Kansas

COLLEGE: Washburn University
                         Curriculum Resources Center
                         1700 College
                         Topeka, KS 66621
                         (913) 295-6300
CONTACT PERSON: Barbara A. Harris
MICROCOMPUTERS: 17 Apple IIe
SOFTWARE TITLES: 120

Kentucky

COLLEGE: Berea College
                         Hutchins Library
                         Berea, KY 40404
                         (606) 986-9341
CONTACT PERSON: Kit Roberts, Cataloger
                         Barbara Power, Circulation
MICROCOMPUTERS: 2 IBM PC, 12 Macintosh, 8 Apple IIe
SOFTWARE TITLES: 279

Massachusetts

COLLEGE: Brandeis University
                         Library
                         Waltham, MA 02254
                         (617) 647-2514
CONTACT PERSON: Carolyn M. Gray, Assistant Director
MICROCOMPUTERS: 14 Macintosh, 2 IBM PC (Main Library)
                         51 IBM PC (Science Library)
SOFTWARE TITLES: 100+

COLLEGE: Bridgewater State College
                         Clement C. Maxwell Library
                         Curriculum Library
                         Bridgewater, MA 02324
                         (617) 697-1304

CONTACT PERSON: Robert M. Simmons
MICROCOMPUTERS: 2 Apple IIe
SOFTWARE TITLES: 100

COLLEGE: Hampshire College
                     Johnson Library Center
                     Amherst, MA 01002
                     (413) 549-4600
CONTACT PERSON: Gai Carpenter, Director
MICROCOMPUTERS: 10 DEC Rainbow, 10 Macintosh
SOFTWARE TITLES: 30+

COLLEGE: Lesley College
                     29 Everett Street
                     Cambridge, MA 02238
                     (617) 868-9600 x161
CONTACT PERSON: Jeff Pankin, Director Computer Lab
MICROCOMPUTERS: 20 Apple IIGS, 20 Apple IIe, 7 IBM PC
SOFTWARE TITLES: 1,000

COLLEGE: Salem State College
                     Library
                     Salem, MA 01970
                     (617) 745-0556
CONTACT PERSON: Glenn Macnutt, Circulation Librarian
MICROCOMPUTERS: 1 Apple
SOFTWARE TITLES: 12

COLLEGE: Simmons College
                     College Library
                     300 The Fenway
                     Boston, MA 02115
                     (617) 738-2242
CONTACT PERSON: Tracey Leger-Hornby, Microcomputer Librarian
MICROCOMPUTERS: 5 Apple IIe, 12 IBM compatibles, 12 Macintosh
SOFTWARE TITLES:

COLLEGE: Springfield College
                     Babson Library
                     262 Alden Street

Springfield, MA 01109
(413) 788-3309
CONTACT PERSON: Gerald Davis, Director
MICROCOMPUTERS: 12 Apple IIe, 4 Zenith
SOFTWARE TITLES: 60

COLLEGE: Suffolk University
Sawyer Library
8 Ashburton Place
Boston, MA 02108
(617) 573-8532
CONTACT PERSON: James R. Coleman
MICROCOMPUTERS: 7 IBM PC
SOFTWARE TITLES: 6

COLLEGE: Westfield State College
Educational Resources Center
Westfield, MA 01086
(413) 568-3311 x2325
CONTACT PERSON: Jeannine Uppgard, Assistant Librarian
MICROCOMPUTERS: 5 DEC Rainbow, 10 Apple IIe, 9 Apple IIc
SOFTWARE TITLES: 110

COLLEGE: Worcester Polytechnic Institute
George C. Gordon Library
100 Institute Road
Worcester, MA 01609
(617) 793-5413
CONTACT PERSON: Helen M. Shuster, Head of Technical Services and Automation
MICROCOMPUTERS: 8 AT&T 6300
SOFTWARE TITLES: 40

Michigan

COLLEGE: Alma College
Library
Alma, MI 48801
(517) 463-7227

CONTACT PERSON: Cathy Palmer
MICROCOMPUTERS: 23 DEC Rainbow
SOFTWARE TITLES: 8

COLLEGE: Michigan State University
                    Audio-Visual Library
                    Main Library Building
                    East Lansing, MI 48824-1048
                    (517) 353-1753
CONTACT PERSON: John D. Shaw
MICROCOMPUTERS: 8 Macintosh, 8 Zenith Z-150
SOFTWARE TITLES: 14

COLLEGE: University of Michigan
                    Undergraduate Library
                    S. University Street
                    Ann Arbor, MI 48109-1185
                    (313) 763-5084
CONTACT PERSON: Barbara MacAdam, Head
MICROCOMPUTERS: 50 Zenith 150, 25 Macintosh
SOFTWARE TITLES: 100+

COLLEGE: University of Michigan—Dearborn
                    Mardigian Library
                    4901 Evergreen
                    Dearborn, MI 48128-1491
                    (313) 593-5400
CONTACT PERSON: Kit Smith, Systems Analyst
MICROCOMPUTERS: 2 Zenith, 2 Macintosh
SOFTWARE TITLES: 7

Mississippi

COLLEGE: Meridian Junior College
                    5500 Highway 19N
                    Meridian, MS 39305
                    (601) 483-8241
CONTACT PERSON: Billy C. Beal

MICROCOMPUTERS: 30 Apple IIe
SOFTWARE TITLES: 9

Missouri

COLLEGE: Southeast Missouri State University
Kent Library
900 Normal
Cape Girardeau, MO 63701
(314) 651-2298
CONTACT PERSON: Jim Eison, Director
Center for Teaching and Learning
MICROCOMPUTERS: 20 IBM PC, 20 Apple IIe
SOFTWARE TITLES: 25

COLLEGE: University of Missouri—Columbia
Ellis Library
Columbia, MO 65201-5149
(314) 882-4701
CONTACT PERSON: Robert A. Almony, Jr.
Assistant Director of Libraries for Administrative Services
MICROCOMPUTERS: 12 Apple, 12 IBM PC
SOFTWARE TITLES: 10+

New Hampshire

COLLEGE: Keene State College
Library
Keene, NH 03431
(603) 352-1909
CONTACT PERSON: Brenda Phillips
MICROCOMPUTERS: 31 Apple IIe
SOFTWARE TITLES: 269

COLLEGE: Plymouth State College
Library

                              Plymouth, NH 03264
                              (603) 536-1550
CONTACT PERSON: Philip Wei, Director
MICROCOMPUTERS: 20 Zenith
SOFTWARE TITLES: 1

New Jersey

COLLEGE: Drew University
                              Madison, NJ 07940
                              (201) 377-3000
CONTACT PERSON: Pamela Snelson
MICROCOMPUTERS: 6 Epson QX-10
SOFTWARE TITLES:

COLLEGE: Rutgers, The State University
                              Alexander Library
                              College Avenue Campus
                              New Brunswick, NJ 08903
                              (201) 932-4822
CONTACT PERSON: Blair C. Brenner, Systems Programmer II/Micros
MICROCOMPUTERS: 6 AT&T 6300, 8 Macintosh 512E
SOFTWARE TITLES: 14

COLLEGE: Rutgers, The State University
                              Douglass Library
                              Douglass Campus
                              New Brunswick, NJ 08903
                              (201) 932-4822
CONTACT PERSON: Blair C. Brenner, Systems Programmer II Micros
MICROCOMPUTERS: 5 Macintosh 512E, 5 AT&T 6300
SOFTWARE TITLES: 14

COLLEGE: Rutgers, The State University
                              Kilmer Library
                              Kilmer Campus
                              Piscataway, NJ 08855
                              (201) 932-4822
CONTACT PERSON: Blair C. Brenner, Systems Programmer II/Micros

MICROCOMPUTERS: 6 Macintosh 512E, 6 AT&T 6300
SOFTWARE TITLES: 14

COLLEGE: Rutgers, The State University
Library of Science and Medicine
POB 1029
Piscataway, NJ 08855-1029
(201) 932-4822
CONTACT PERSON: Blair C. Brenner, Systems Programmer II/Micros
MICROCOMPUTERS: 6 Macintosh 512E, 6 AT&T 6300
SOFTWARE TITLES: 14

COLLEGE: Seton Hall University
McLaughlin Library
400 South Orange Avenue
South Orange, NJ 07079
(201) 761-9005
CONTACT PERSON: Gen McGinn, Circulation Librarian
MICROCOMPUTERS: 4 IBM XT, 2 IBM PC
SOFTWARE TITLES: 2

New York

COLLEGE: Adelphi University
Swirbul Library
Garden City, NY 11530
(516) 663-1032
CONTACT PERSON: Rochelle Sager
MICROCOMPUTERS: 5 TI, 5 Apple II
SOFTWARE TITLES:

COLLEGE: Cornell University
Mann Library
Ithaca, NY 14853
(607) 255-3240
CONTACT PERSON: Gwen Urey, Microcomputer Center Manager
MICROCOMPUTERS: 29 IBM PC, 5 Macintosh, 1 DEC Rainbow
SOFTWARE TITLES: 170

COLLEGE: Nazareth College of Rochester
                            Lorette Wilmot Library
                            4245 East Avenue
                            Rochester, NY 14610
                            (716) 586-2525
CONTACT PERSON: Richard Matzek, Director
MICROCOMPUTERS: 10 Apple II+/e, 8 Macintosh
SOFTWARE TITLES: 100+

COLLEGE: New York University
                            Bobst Library
                            70 Washington Square South
                            New York, NY 10012
                            (212) 998-2585
CONTACT PERSON: Michael D. Miller, Head
                            Avery Fisher Center for Music and Media
MICROCOMPUTERS: 11 Macintosh
SOFTWARE TITLES: 2

COLLEGE: Rensselaer Polytechnic Institute
                            Folsom Library
                            Troy, NY 12180-3590
                            (518) 276-8320
CONTACT PERSON: Polly-Alida Farrington, Software Consultant
MICROCOMPUTERS: 20 IBM PC, 10 Mac Plus
SOFTWARE TITLES: 850

COLLEGE: St. John Fisher College
                            Lavery Library
                            3690 East Avenue
                            Rochester, NY 14618
                            (716) 385-8382
CONTACT PERSON: Ling-Ling Lee, Coordinator of Online Library Sys-
                            tems
MICROCOMPUTERS: 20 Zenith
SOFTWARE TITLES: 19

COLLEGE: State University of New York–Cortland

Memorial Library
POB 2000
Cortland, NY 13045
(607) 753-2221

CONTACT PERSON: Selby U. Gration, Director
MICROCOMPUTERS: 26 Apple IIe, 1 PC Junior, 3 Zenith, 1 TRS-80,
                    Commodore 64

SOFTWARE TITLES: 55

COLLEGE: State University of New York–Geneseo
                    Fraser Library
                    Geneseo, NY 14454
                    (716) 245-5334

CONTACT PERSON: Paul MacLean, Managing Librarian
MICROCOMPUTERS: 43 Apple IIe, 12 Macintosh, 24 IBM PC
SOFTWARE TITLES: 180

COLLEGE: University of Rochester
                    Rush Rhees Library
                    Rochester, NY 14627
                    (716) 275-4461

CONTACT PERSON: Michael Poulin
                    Diane J. Reiman
MICROCOMPUTERS: 20 IBM PC, 8 Macintosh
SOFTWARE TITLES: 19

North Carolina

COLLEGE: University of North Carolina
                    Health Sciences Library
                    Learning Resources Center
                    Chapel Hill, NC 27514
                    (919) 962-0600

CONTACT PERSON: Diane Foxman, Head
MICROCOMPUTERS: 10 IBM PC, 6 Macintosh Plus
SOFTWARE TITLES: 400

COLLEGE: University of North Carolina at Charlotte

	J. Murrey Atkins Library
	UNCC Station
	Charlotte, NC 28223
	(704) 547-2559
CONTACT PERSON:	Judith A. Walker
MICROCOMPUTERS:	IBM PC, Apple
SOFTWARE TITLES:	

COLLEGE:	Wingate College
	Ethel K. Smith Library
	200 Elm Street
	Wingate, NC 28174-0217
	(704) 233-4061
CONTACT PERSON:	Mark Seagroves, Director of Academic Computing
MICROCOMPUTERS:	24 Apple IIe
SOFTWARE TITLES:	40

North Dakota

COLLEGE:	North Dakota State University
	Library
	Fargo, ND 58102
	(701) 237-8876
CONTACT PERSON:	Douglas Birdsall, Head of Public Services
MICROCOMPUTERS:	Zenith, IBM PC
SOFTWARE TITLES:	50+

COLLEGE:	University of North Dakota
	Chester Fritz Library
	Grand Forks, ND 58202
	(701) 777-4637
CONTACT PERSON:	Jon Boone, Coordinator of Collection Development
MICROCOMPUTERS:	8 IBM PC, 9 Apple IIe, 2 Macintosh
SOFTWARE TITLES:	150

Ohio

COLLEGE:	Bowling Green State University

	Bowling Green, OH 43403
	(419) 372-2856
CONTACT PERSON:	Bonnie Gratch
MICROCOMPUTERS:	20 IBM PC, 15 Macintosh, 2 Apple II
SOFTWARE TITLES:	

COLLEGE:	Raymond Walters College
	University of Cincinnati
	9555 Plainfield Road
	Cincinnati, OH 45236
	(513) 745-4313
CONTACT PERSON:	Lucy Wilson
MICROCOMPUTERS:	30 IBM PC
SOFTWARE TITLES:	160

Pennsylvania

COLLEGE:	Carnegie Mellon University
	Hunt Library
	5000 Forbes Avenue
	Pittsburgh, PA 15213
	(412) 268-3386
CONTACT PERSON:	Ida Joiner
MICROCOMPUTERS:	2 IBM PC, 1 Macintosh XL, 1 MicroVAX II, 8 IBM RT/PC, 40 Macintosh
SOFTWARE TITLES:	400

COLLEGE:	Hahnemann University
	Library
	15th and Vine Streets
	Philadelphia, PA 19102
	(215) 448-7269
CONTACT PERSON:	Sharon Dennis, Manager
	Microcomputer Laboratory
MICROCOMPUTERS:	1 Macintosh SE, 9 Compaq Deskpro, 6 IBM PC XT, 1 IBM PC AT
SOFTWARE TITLES:	35

COLLEGE: Lehigh University
                      Fairchild Martindale Library
                      Bethlehem, PA 18015
                      (215) 758-3075
CONTACT PERSON: Sharon L. Siegler, Associate Director, Public Services
MICROCOMPUTERS: 75 Zenith 158-42
SOFTWARE TITLES: 14

COLLEGE: Mansfield University
                      Main Library
                      Mansfield, PA 16933
                      (717) 662-4071
CONTACT PERSON: Martha Donahue
MICROCOMPUTERS: 28 IBM PC
SOFTWARE TITLES:

COLLEGE: Pennsylvania State University
                      Pattee Library
                      University Park, PA 16802
                      (814) 865-0401
CONTACT PERSON: James G. Neal, Assistant Dean and Head Reference and
                      Instructional Services Division
MICROCOMPUTERS: 10 Macintosh Plus, 10 IBM PS2
SOFTWARE TITLES:

COLLEGE: Pennsylvania State University
                      Berks Campus
                      POB 7009
                      Reading, PA 19610-6009
CONTACT PERSON: Sally S. Small, Head Librarian
MICROCOMPUTERS: 2 Apple IIe, 4 AT&T, 4 IBM PC
SOFTWARE TITLES: 30

COLLEGE: Philadelphia College of Pharmacy & Science
                      J. W. England Library
                      4200 Woodland Avenue
                      Philadelphia, PA 19104
                      (215) 596-8993
CONTACT PERSON: Joyce Zogott, Head
                      Learning Resources Center

MICROCOMPUTERS: 2 IBM PC XT, 3 Macintosh
SOFTWARE TITLES: 25
COLLEGE: Slippery Rock University
    Bailey Library
    Slippery Rock, PA 16057
    (412) 794-7243
CONTACT PERSON: Jane Scott, IMC Librarian
MICROCOMPUTERS: 3 IBM PC
SOFTWARE TITLES: 32

COLLEGE: Ursinus College
    Myrin Library
    Main Street
    Collegeville, PA 19426
    (215) 489-4111 x2243
CONTACT PERSON: Charles A. Jamison, Director
MICROCOMPUTERS: 25 Leading Edge Model D
SOFTWARE TITLES: 15

COLLEGE: West Chester University
    Francis Harvey Green Library
    Rosedale & High Streets
    West Chester, PA 19383
    (215) 436-3477/78
CONTACT PERSON: Janet Tordone, Administrative Assistant
MICROCOMPUTERS: 40 Apple IIc/e/GS, Macintosh, IBM
SOFTWARE TITLES: 1000

Rhode Island

COLLEGE: Rhode Island College
    Curriculum Resources Center
    600 Mt. Pleasant Avenue
    Providence, RI 02908
    (401) 462-8052
CONTACT PERSON: Maureen T. Lapan, Director
MICROCOMPUTERS: 2 IBM PC, 1 Apple II+, 1 Apple IIc, 2 Macintosh, 1
    PC Jr., 2 TRS-80, 3 Atari, 1 Commodore, 1 Amiga,

	1 Bell & Howell
SOFTWARE TITLES:	720

South Dakota

COLLEGE:	University of South Dakota
	I.D. Weeks Library
	414 E. Clark Street
	Vermillion, SD 57069
	(605) 677-5371
CONTACT PERSON:	Karen Zimmerman, Librarian
	Learning Resources
MICROCOMPUTERS:	3 Apple II, 1 Apple IIe, 1 Apple IIGS, 10 Kaypro PC
SOFTWARE TITLES:	215

Texas

COLLEGE:	Austin College
	Abell Library Center
	Sherman, TX 75090
	(214) 892-9101
CONTACT PERSON:	Nell Evans, Systems Librarian
MICROCOMPUTERS:	21 IBM PC XT
SOFTWARE TITLES:	28

COLLEGE:	North Texas State University
	Media Library
	POB 12898
	Denton, TX 76203
	(817) 565-2489
CONTACT PERSON:	George Mitchell, Media Library Director
MICROCOMPUTERS:	1 Apple IIe, 2 TI-PC
SOFTWARE TITLES:	136

COLLEGE:	Southern Methodist University
	Central University Libraries
	Dallas, TX 75275
	(214) 692-2400
CONTACT PERSON:	Linda Sellers

MICROCOMPUTERS: 2 Macintosh
SOFTWARE TITLES:

COLLEGE: Texas A&M University
Evans Library
Learning Resources Department
College Station, TX 77843
(409) 845-2316
CONTACT PERSON: Hal W. Hall, Head
Special Formats Division
MICROCOMPUTERS: 9 Apple IIe, 44 IBM PC, 2 Compaq, 9 Macintosh SE
SOFTWARE TITLES: 500+

COLLEGE: Texas Tech University
University Library
Lubbock, TX 79409
(806) 742-1926
CONTACT PERSON: Jennifer Cargill, Associate Director of Libraries for In-
formation Access and Systems
MICROCOMPUTERS: 25 TI 99/4A
SOFTWARE TITLES:

COLLEGE: University of Houston
4800 Calhoun
Houston, TX 77004
(713) 749-4241
CONTACT PERSON: Judy Myers
MICROCOMPUTERS: 5 IBM XT
SOFTWARE TITLES:

COLLEGE: University of Texas at Austin
General Libraries
Austin, TX 78713
(512) 471-3811
CONTACT PERSON: Mary Seng
MICROCOMPUTERS: 11 IBM PC
SOFTWARE TITLES: 49

COLLEGE: University of Texas at Dallas
P.O. Box 643

	Richardson, TX 75080
	(214) 690-2950
CONTACT PERSON:	Abby Kratz
MICROCOMPUTERS:	1 Apple II, 3 Control Data 100, 1 TRS 80, 1 Eagle II
SOFTWARE TITLES:	

Vermont

COLLEGE:	University of Vermont
	Bailey/Howe Library
	University of Vermont
	Burlington, VT 05405
	(802) 656-2020
CONTACT PERSON:	Wesley Eldred, Library Supervisor
MICROCOMPUTERS:	35 AT&T
SOFTWARE TITLES:	9

Virginia

COLLEGE:	Christopher Newport College
	Captain John Smith Library
	50 Shoe Lane
	Newport News, VA 23606
	(804) 599-7130
CONTACT PERSON:	Hugh Treacy
MICROCOMPUTERS:	1 Apple II, 1 IBM PC
SOFTWARE TITLES:	

COLLEGE:	Hampden-Sydney College
	Eggleston Library
	P.O. Box 7
	Hampden-Sydney, VA 23943
	(804) 223-4381
CONTACT PERSON:	David J. Norden, Director
MICROCOMPUTERS:	8 Macintosh
SOFTWARE TITLES:	50

Washington

COLLEGE: Eastern Washington University
                      University Library
                      Cheney, WA 99004
                      (509) 359-7048
CONTACT PERSON: Ted Otto, Assistant University Librarian for Public
                      Services
MICROCOMPUTERS: 2 Apple
SOFTWARE TITLES: 300+

Wisconsin

COLLEGE: University of Wisconsin–Parkside
                      Library/Learning Center
                      POB 2000
                      Kenosha, WI 53141
                      (414) 553-2642
CONTACT PERSON: Linda Piele, Associate Director
MICROCOMPUTERS: 8 Apple II+, 9 Apple IIe, 16 IBM PC, 18 Zenith, 11
                      Macintosh
SOFTWARE TITLES: 400

COLLEGE: University of Wisconsin–Whitewater Andersen Library
                      800 W. Main Street
                      Whitewater, WI 53190
                      (414) 472-1000
CONTACT PERSON: Joyce Huang
MICROCOMPUTERS: 6 Apple II, 2 Macintosh, 2 IBM PC
SOFTWARE TITLES: 410

About the Contributors

MARY LOUISE BRADY received her master's degree in library science from Rosary College in River Forest, Illinois, in 1966, and her master's degree in education from the California Polytechnic State University, San Luis Obispo, in 1978. She has been a librarian at Cal Poly since 1968, and is presently the head of the Learning Resources and Curriculum Department of the Robert E. Kennedy Library, and the director of the Curriculum Micro Center, which is part of the LR & C Department. She also serves as director of San Luis Obispo County's Instructional Materials Display Center for the California State Deparment of Education.

LISA CAMARDO is currently the microcomputer coordinator for South-Western Publishing Company, an educational media and textbook publisher in Cincinnati, Ohio. Prior to her appointment there, she spent three years at the University of Cincinnati as the coordinator of computer support services at Raymond Walters College. Ms. Camardo earned her bachelor's degree in elementary education and a master of arts in instructional design and technology from the Ohio State University. She has served as a computer consultant for such organizations as the Columbus, Ohio, public school system, the Indian Hill Exempted School Village in Cincinnati, and PepsiCo.

MAUREEN T. LAPAN, Ph.D., has been a professor of education at Rhode Island College since 1966, and is the director of the Rhode Island College Curriculum Resources Center. She also teaches courses in curriculum theory and research, foundations of education, and curriculum design. Dr. Lapan has served as a consultant to curriculum development projects in the United States, the Republic of Ireland, and the United Kingdom, has authored articles, and has presented conference papers, including "Microcomputer Software as Curriculum Content: Some Observations."

PAUL MACLEAN has been a librarian at the State University of New York, College at Geneseo, since 1979. For five years he has been the managing librarian at Fraser Library, a branch library for business, computer science, and mathematics. Fraser Library is also the location of the college's main microcomputer lab. From 1975 through 1979, Mr. MacLean worked in various positions at the Harvard Business School's Baker Library. During this time, he studied at Simmons College for a master's degree in library science, which he received in 1979. He graduated in 1965 from Yale University, where his major was American studies.

LINDA PIELE received her bachelor's degree in French from the University of Washington, her master's degree in French from the University of Oregon, and her master's degree in library science from the University of Wisconsin-Milwaukee. She has been at the University of Wisconsin-Parkside Library/Learning Center since 1976, presently serving as the associate director for public services. Ms. Piele has co-authored two books, *Communication Research: Strategies and Sources* (Wadsworth, 1976) and *Materials and Methods for Business Research* (Neal-Schuman, 1980), as well as several articles concerning microcomputer labs in academic libraries. She has been active in the Association of College and Research Libraries since 1979 and chaired that group's Microcomputer Services in Academic Libraries Discussion Group from 1984 to 1986.

PEGGY SEIDEN received a bachelor's degree from Colby College, a master's degree in medieval studies from the University of Toronto, and a master's degree in library science from Rutgers University. She is currently the software manager for academic computing at Carnegie-Mellon University and previously served there as the librarian for educational computing. In that position, she was responsible for the development and management of the educational software library and associated computing clusters. Ms. Seiden is the leader of the EDUCOM Software Initiative Task Group on Information Resources and also chairs the Association of College and Research Libraries' Microcomputer Services in Academic Libraries Discussion Group.

JEANNINE UPPGARD received her bachelor's degree from Rivier College, her master's degree in library science from SUNY-Geneseo, and her master's degree in business administration from Western New England College. Since 1976, she has been a librarian at Westfield State College in Massachusetts, where she is the director of the Educational Resources Center, a curriculum collection that supports the undergraduate and graduate programs offered by the college's Education Department. Since 1983 the ERC has provided a microcomputer lab and software collection as part of its services. Ms. Uppgard has authored an article, "Public Access Microcomputers in Academic Libraries," in *Small Computers in Libraries*, volume 7, numbers 1 and 2 (1987).

Index